Contents

1   **The philosophy**   2

2   **Energy and feng shui**   20

3   **Putting feng shui into practice**   28

4   **Feng shui and houses**   48

5   **Applying feng shui**   66

1

the
philosophy

This chapter introduces Taoism, the ancient Chinese religion, and its central concept of ch'i. Ch'i is the universal energy which flows through and around ourselves, our homes, our workplaces and surroundings.

Feng shui is about how ch'i flows, its strengths and weaknesses, how to improve its flow, how to control and direct it and how to make maximum use of the life-giving power it brings to us. The principles of feng shui are based in the Taoist concepts of heaven and earth, of yin and yang, of the four seasons, of the eight compass point and of the five elements – fire, water, metal, wood and earth. These different aspects of the world combine and interact in a number of ways, the most important of which is the PahKwa, or Great Symbol. The PahKwa is central to how feng shui practitioners view spaces.

What is feng shui?

Feng shui is a subtle art whereby we can change our environment to alter our luck, health, wealth and love life. This may involve reorganizing your entire house or merely changing where you site your desk or hanging a few mirrors in a window. As we will see in this book, the subtle change can be the one to make the most impact.

The Chinese have known and practised feng shui for around 5,000 years and during that time they have had plenty of opportunity to observe the art in action to see if it actually has any benefit or positive results; if it hadn't, they would have stopped doing it long before now. The fact that they haven't seems to indicate there may be something to it.

If we live our lives subject to the random forces of the universe we can't complain if we seem to suffer bad luck, misfortune, ill health and random acts of disaster. If, however, by using feng shui we decide to take responsibility and control of our lives, we must surely see only an improvement. Feng shui is about taking control, taking responsibility.

Feng shui teaches us to look at every facet of our lives and question them. Are we as happy with every aspect as we might be? If we aren't then by following the principles of feng shui we can make changes. Perhaps the results of these changes cannot be as accurately predicted as we might wish but by making changes we are taking control. All the theory in the world won't change a single thing – only by actually doing something will we learn, understand and cause change. As an old Chinese sage once said:

I hear and I forget
I see and I remember
I do and I understand.

These changes are, in themselves, tiny but it is the fact that we are actually doing something, wresting control from fate and bestowing it upon ourselves, that has an effect. The change might appear insignificant – moving a plant, placing a mirror, hanging a wind-chime – but the results could be enormous and, of course, beneficial.

Suppose, for example, you casually throw a stick into a river. It catches on a submerged tree stump. Your stick collects other twigs and floating flotsam. This collection of debris gets bigger, becomes a dam, the river floods the neighbouring fields, drowns the livestock, forces the farmer to higher ground to take refuge, activates the emergency services. And all because you casually tossed a stick into a river.

Now suppose the river was ch'i, the universal energy, and it had flooded to such an extent that it was adversely affecting your life. A feng shui consultant might say 'remove that tiny stick'. You might think it wouldn't make any difference – after all, your emotional fields are flooded, your mental livestock are drowned, your internal farmer seems to have escaped you and your emergency services (nerves) are activated – your life is dammed and flooded. You, cynically and unwillingly, remove the stick. The debris is free to wash away, the river returns to its normal course, the fields dry out and everything returns to normal – and all because you removed a tiny stick that was clogging things up.

This example may appear trivial or irrelevant but that is how feng shui works. We clog up our lives with pieces of furniture in the wrong place or an ill-advised location for our house, or a sticking door that is hampering the good flow of ch'i. Once we unclog or remove the debris, the ch'i can flow properly again and life returns to normal. Perhaps, by the judicious placing of a fresh stick, we might even improve things.

Feng shui is about how ch'i flows, its strengths and weaknesses, how to improve its flow, how to control and direct it and how to make maximum use of the life-giving power it brings to us.

A brief outline of Taoism

To understand the principles of feng shui we have to have an understanding of Taoism, the ancient religion of China.

Taoism comes from the *Tao* (pronounced: dow), which can be translated, and understood, as the Way.

The Chinese say that everything is the Tao, everything is the Way. The Tao cannot really be likened to our Western concept of God except that it is all-pervading, always present, in everything and without end. The fundamental difference is that the Tao has no direct personality – it just *is*. It has no gender or agenda; no divine plan or sense of morality or sin.

From the Tao, the Way, comes everything we can know. That everything, according to Taoists, can be divided into heaven and creation, or spirit and matter. Taoists represented heaven as a circle and creation, surrounded on all sides by heaven, as a square (see Figure 1). This is a fundamental symbol often encountered in Chinese art – it is still depicted on lucky coins among the Chinese today.

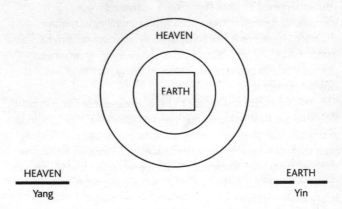

Figure 1 *Heaven and earth.*

From heaven, or spirit, the Taoists reduced the circle to an unbroken line called yang, while creation, or matter, became a broken line called yin. The yin/yang symbolism was further developed into the best-known of all Chinese symbols (see Figure 2).

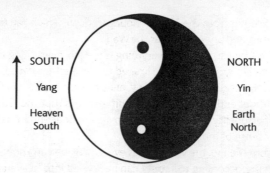

SOUTH
Yang
Heaven
South

NORTH
Yin
Earth
North

Figure 2 *The yin/yang symbol.*

This is sometimes known as the T'ai Ch'i, the Supreme Ultimate or the Great Art. From the Supreme Ultimate there comes the Tao, from the Tao comes yang and yin and from those two opposites there is everything in balance. Although the yang and yin are opposites, within each there is always an element of the other. This is why there is always the tiny dot of white within the black yin, and the tiny dot of dark within the white of the yang. These two opposites are constantly being reborn as each other – in a state of constant flux and movement – and this movement between the two is what gives birth to the flow of energy, ch'i. You might like to think of it as the flow of alternating current electricity.

Yang and yin possess their own qualities and are given aspects and attitudes, but remember that this is only their basic character – they are always changing to their opposite polarization.

The list below is by no means exhaustive: everything in heaven and earth is classified as either yin or yang. The problem most Westerners have with this is that they tend to see yin and yang as two opposites; something is yin/female or something is yang/male, whereas the Chinese are always aware of the seed of the yang in the yin and the seed of the yin in the yang: nothing is ever only one or the other, there is always a balance within the thing itself.

Yin	Yang
female	male
receptive	creative
dark	light
night	day
soft	hard
down	up
north	south
matter	spirit
earth	sky
negative	positive
passive	active
wet	dry
winter	summer

The yin/yang symbol should always be shown with the yin to the right, as shown in Figure 2. This is the basis of compass directions. The light yang is at the top representing summer and the south, while the dark yin is at the bottom representing winter and the north. All Chinese compasses are the opposite way round to those in the West: they have their south at the top, west to the right, etc (see Figure 3).

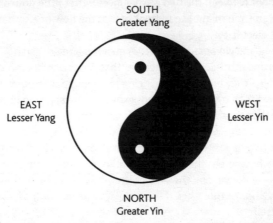

SOUTH
Greater Yang

EAST
Lesser Yang

WEST
Lesser Yin

NORTH
Greater Yin

Figure 3 *Yin/Yang with compass directions.*

The yin/yang symbol can also be used to represent the human body, with the head at the top representing spirit, yang, and the body below representing matter, yin. Yang is the left-hand side of the body, representing male, while the right-hand side, yin, represents female (see Figure 4).

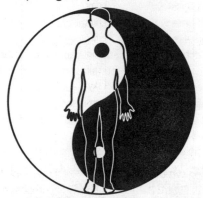

Figure 4 *Yin/Yang and the human body.*

The four seasons

The symbols for yin, north, and yang, south, can be combined to create another two to represent east and west, spring and autumn (see Figure 5).

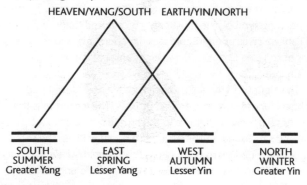

Figure 5 *The four lines.*

The eight trigrams

From these four new symbols another four can be produced
to give the rest of the compass and the mid-season points
(see Figure 6). These are known as the eight trigrams (a trigram
is three parallel lines).

* The top lines represent the duality of heaven and
  creation – the yin/yang.
* The middle lines represent heaven and creation coming
  together to create the four seasons and the cardinal points
  of the compass.
* The bottom lines represent humans.

The eight trigrams are all named and have various significance
and attributes. Each is listed below by its Chinese name, with its
translation, main attribute, direction and season.

* **Ch'ien** – *The Creative*, heaven, south, summer
* **Tui** – *The Lake*, metal, south-east, joy
* **Li** – *The Clinging* – fire, east, the sun, spring
* **Chen** – *The Arousing*, wood, north-east, thunder
* **K'un** – *The Receptive*, creation, north, winter
* **Ken** – *The Stillness*, mountain, north-west, calm
* **K'an** – *The Dangerous*, water, west, the moon, autumn
* **H'sun** – *The Gentle*, wind, south-west, wood

We can now form these trigrams into an octagon known as
the *PahKwa*, the Great Symbol (Figure 7), which is probably, after
the yin/yang symbol, the most easily recognized Chinese art form.
The PahKwa gives us eight compass directions, eight seasons, eight
types of ch'i (see Chapter 2) and eight areas of life or enrichments
(see Chapter 3).

The eight trigrams are thought to have been developed by
Fu His, a Chinese emperor, around 3000 BC. The legend tells that
he first saw the eight trigrams in the ornate markings of a tortoise
shell which he found on the banks of the Yellow River. The sequence
in which he found them is known as the *Former Heaven Sequence*.
Around 1000 BC they were rearranged into a different sequence,
called the *Later Heaven Sequence*, by Emperor Wen, who was both a

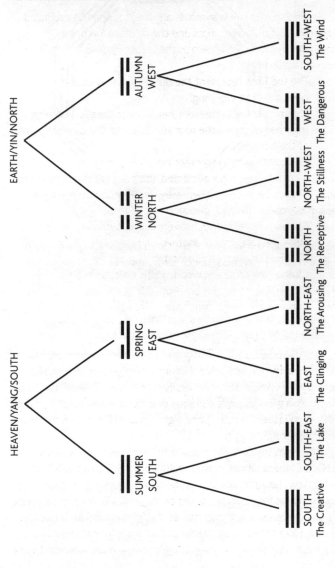

Figure 6 *The eight trigrams.*

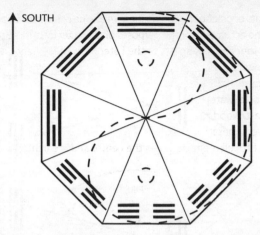

↑ SOUTH

Figure 7 *The PahKwa, the Great Symbol.*

philosopher and the founder of the Chou Dynasty. We use only the original Former Heaven Sequence for feng shui.

The I Ching

The eight trigrams can be paired into 64 new symbols (8 multiplied by 8) called *hexagrams*, which use six lines. These 64 hexagrams each have a meaning; Fu His wrote about them and used them first as an agricultural almanac, which he called the *I Ching* (pronounced: eeching), the Book of Changes. As this was some 5,000 years ago, the I Ching is probably the oldest book in existence. Emperor Wen added to Fu His's interpretations and turned it into the I Ching as we know it.

The five elements

Most Oriental wisdom, medicine and philosophy, including feng shui, is based on the Theory of the Five Aspects (*Wu Hsing*), which says that, while we are a combination of all the elements or aspects, we do tend to display predominantly the characteristics of one over the others. These elements are a sort of shorthand whereby feng shui consultants or practitioners of Chinese medicine could sum up a person quickly and accurately for the purposes of character identification.

The four cardinal points of the Later Heaven Sequence are also four elements:

* south/fire
* north/water
* east/wood
* west/metal.

The fifth element occupies the centre and is earth.

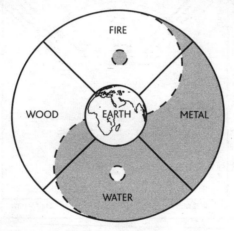

Figure 8 *The five elements with earth in the centre.*

These five elements are incorporated into compass directions and human characteristics. This is why the five elements are so important to practitioners of feng shui. A consultant would want to see your house *and* know your date of birth. From the date, the consultant knows which of the animals in Chinese astrology you are. Each of these 12 animals has five different aspects – the natural element, which is based on the year you were born. Thus you are never just a tiger or dog or dragon but maybe a metal tiger, an earth dog or a water dragon.

Once a consultant knows which element you are, they can work out which direction suits you best. Perhaps you need to know which animal you are, as these too have their own compass directions as well as best seasons, times of day, key words and colours.

Chinese animals and their key words

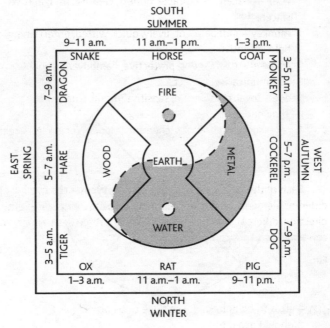

Figure 9 *The animals and the elements.*

* rat – ambitious, hardworking, determined, industrious, intelligent, practical
* ox – patient, courageous, conventional, reliable, purposeful, intelligent
* tiger – daring, entertaining, exhausting, passionate, dangerous, hasty
* hare – generous, intuitive, tactile, egotistical, discreet
* dragon – enthusiastic, daring, inspiring, successful, materialistic, independent

* snake – intelligent, mysterious, intuitive, daring, ordered, sophisticated
* horse – loyal, hardworking, gregarious, friendly, energetic, well-liked
* goat – peaceful, adaptable, honest, creative, imaginative, sincere
* monkey – independent, lively, quick-witted, entertaining, bold, inventive
* cockerel – courageous, protective, flamboyant, capable, communicative, honest
* dog – loyal, responsible, sensitive, moral, trustworthy, imaginative
* pig – sensual, generous, cheerful, tolerant, fortunate, eager

Characteristics of the five elements

Each of the 12 animals has five distinct types – the five different elements – and each elemental type favours a different direction, different season and even different remedies to apply to correct any corrupt ch'i (*sha*).

Fire
* compassionate, intuitive, communicative
* likes pleasure, seeks excitement
* likes to be in love, doesn't like to be bored
* should avoid heat

Water
* imaginative, honest, clever
* seeks knowledge, original, tough, independent
* can be secretive, needs to be protected
* should avoid cold

Metal
* organized, likes to control, precise, discriminating
* needs to be right, likes order and cleanliness
* appreciates quality
* should avoid dryness

Wood
* expansive, purposeful, active
* likes to be busy, can be domineering
* needs to win, practical
* should avoid windy environments

Earth
* moderate, sense of loyalty, harmonious
* likes to belong, pays attention to detail
* likes company, needs to be needed
* can be stubborn
* should avoid damp

Natural elements

Each animal has its *natural element* of which only four are used (not earth) and each animal has its *year element* of which there are five. Each year also has its element and its yin or yang quality. Each animal has its qualities, based on these elements, and needs a different living location if it is to thrive and prosper.

Elements and houses

Element	Ideal house	Good interior colours	Key word
Fire	north facing, comfortable, warm but quite grand, like a manor house	reds, oranges	enthusiasm
Water	south facing, older more traditional house, like a period thatched cottage	black, dark blues	hope
Metal	east facing, modern, designer house	white, grey, pale blues	organization
Earth	a mid-terrace or a basement flat but it would have to be family oriented – perhaps a farmhouse	yellow, ochre, rust and brown	caring

The *natural* elements for the 12 animals are:
* water (north) – pig, rat and ox
* metal (west) – dog, cockerel and monkey
* fire (south) – goat, horse and snake
* wood (east) – tiger, hare and dragon.

An animal's *natural* element is different from the *year* element. Suppose, for example, you were born in 1965 – that would make you a yin wood snake. But a snake *naturally* is a fire animal. Wood is happiest in the west (its opposite aspect) and fire happiest in the north (its opposite aspect). If you were born in 1965, you may find your best direction would be a north-west facing home, thus combining your wood and fire elements.

We look to site our home in our opposite aspect to calm down the ch'i or enliven it. For example, a fire type would seek a north-facing home to calm down the invigorating southern ch'i. A water type would seek a south-facing home so they wouldn't be swamped by all the protective sleepy northern ch'i.

The four compass directions

These four compass directions are important and we should look at them in some detail.

South
* Symbolized by the *phoenix*, known as the Red Bird of the South.
* The phoenix is called *Feng Huang* (it can also be a pheasant, cockerel or any bright bird).
* The south represents luck, the summer, fame and fortune, happiness, light, joy and hope.
* Its element is fire.
* Animals – goat, horse, snake.
* Season – summer.
* The ch'i that comes from the south is *invigorating*.

North

* Symbolized by the Black Tortoise.
* The tortoise is called *Yuan Wu* (can also be a coiled snake, a turtle, a black warrior and even smoke).
* The north represents the hidden, the mysterious, winter, sleep, ritual, nurture and caring.
* The north's colour is black.
* Its element is water.
* Animals — pig, rat, ox.
* Season — winter.
* The ch'i from the north is *protective* and *nurturing*.

East

* Symbolized by the Green Dragon.
* The dragon is called *Wen* (can also be gold but always a dragon).
* The east is protective, cultured, wise, spring, kindness and learning.
* The east's colour is green.
* Its element is wood.
* Animals — tiger, hare, dragon.
* Season — spring.
* The ch'i from the east is *expansive* and *mature*.

West

* Symbolized by the White Tiger.
* The tiger is called *Wu*.
* The west is an area of unpredictability, even danger.
* It contains warfare and strength, the autumn, anger, suddenness and potential violence.
* The west's colour is white.
* Its element is metal.
* Animals — dog, cockerel, monkey.
* Season — autumn.
* The ch'i from the west is *unpredictable*.

The four quadrantal points

The Chinese think in terms of eight compass directions; the second four – south-east, south-west, north-east, north-west – are equally important to feng shui. They are known as the four *quadrantal* compass points.

* **South-east** – combines the vigorous ch'i of the south with the growing ch'i of the east to produce its own unique *creative ch'i*.

* **South-west** – combines the vigorous south ch'i with the changeable ch'i of the west to produce *soothing ch'i*.

* **North-east** – combines the nurturing ch'i of the north with the growing ch'i of the east to produce *flourishing ch'i*.

* **North-west** – combines the nurturing ch'i of the north with the changeable ch'i of the west to produce *expansive ch'i*.

As we gain or suffer depending on what sort of ch'i is arriving on our doorstep it is important to know what direction our house faces and thus what sort of ch'i will be dominating our lives.

Once we know which way our house faces we can begin to determine which ch'i, and which quality, will dominate in our home. You may need a small compass to work out your direction.

energy and feng shui

Feng shui is all about the energy of ch'i – how it flows, how it gets blocked, how it can become corrupted and stagnate – and what these things can mean for us.

Ch'i energy is universal; it has seasons and a flow; it has form, movement and qualities. The calligraphy for ch'i is the same as for 'rice'. Rice and ch'i are the great universal life-givers to the Chinese. Ch'i also plays a great part in traditional Chinese medicine. Internal ch'i has several different forms: guarding ch'i, protein ch'i, original ch'i and protective ch'i. If the internal ch'i stagnates or gets misdirected it causes illness. This illness is treated usually by acupuncture, which corrects the flow of ch'i by placing tiny needles into strategic meridian points in the body.

Ch'i is not only internal. External ch'i is affected by the direction it comes from, weather, seasonal changes and atmospheric conditions.

Ch'i and sha

If you imagine standing in the middle of your home, you can turn in eight different compass directions and you will receive the benefit of the eight different types of ch'i. What if the ch'i was failing on its way to you and becoming *sha*? There are eight different types of sha depending on which direction it comes from.

Ch'i is living, bringing good energy, whereas sha is ch'i that is stagnant or corrupt and it can bring ill health, bad luck, a loss of fortune, arguments, depression and negative energy.

The true art of feng shui is interpreting the sha and making changes to our environment that cause the sha to become ch'i again.

* **South.** *Vigorous ch'i* degrades to *accelerating sha* which causes you to feel exhausted.
* **North.** *Nurturing ch'i* degrades to *lingering sha* which causes you to feel lethargic.
* **East.** *Growing ch'i* degrades to *overpowering sha* which causes you to feel egotistical and vain.
* **West.** *Changeable ch'i* degrades to *dangerous sha* which causes you to act rashly.
* **South-east.** *Creative ch'i* degrades to *provoking sha* which causes you to feel irritable and headachy.
* **South-west.** *Soothing ch'i* degrades to *disruptive sha* which causes you to feel angry.
* **North-east.** *Flourishing ch'i* degrades to *stagnating sha* which causes ill health.
* **North-west.** *Expansive ch'i* degrades to *unpredictable sha* which causes you to feel unsettled.

Figure 10 shows how these eight directions receive their ch'i. You will notice that there is a movement from spring/east through summer/south to autumn/west and finally to winter/north.

The movement of ch'i

There is a logical flow of ch'i:
* it starts as growing ch'i in the spring (east)
* becomes vigorous ch'i in the summer (south)

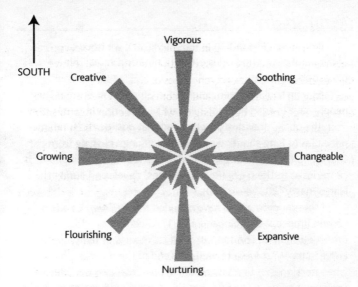

Figure 10 Ch'i directions.

* becomes changeable ch'i in the autumn (west)
* and settles to sleepy nurturing ch'i in the winter (north).

The colours also follow a pattern:
* green in the spring to represent growth
* red in the summer for heat
* white in the autumn for mists and frosts
* black in the winter for sleep and hibernation.

This also gives us a cycle for the five elements:
* wood helps fire
* fire helps earth (the centre)
* earth helps metal
* metal helps water
* water helps wood.

Each of these creates the next in the cycle – but it can also hinder it if the flow is incorrect.

Feng shui in China

Before we can start to practise feng shui we need to understand how feng shui is used in China and what Chinese philosophy is about.

As feng shui has been practised in China for at least as long as people have lived in houses, there are several ancient texts apart from the books previously mentioned that outline the fundamental principles of feng shui and explain its workings, ranging from the *Shih Ching* (Book of Songs) compiled between the ninth and fifth centuries BC to the *Li Chi* (Record of Rites) developed during the Han dynasty (206 BC–AD 220).

More modern works have included the *Ku Chin T'uShu Chi Ch'eng* (Imperial Encyclopaedia), a 1726 edition of which is in the British Museum in London, but the first reports of feng shui to arrive in the West were towards the end of the nineteenth century when missionaries first visited China on a regular basis. They were somewhat surprised to find that there was already an ancient and well-developed religion in place, Taoism, which was closely bound up with feng shui, and were somewhat taken aback when they were not allowed to erect Christian crosses. It was bad feng shui, they were told, to stab the land.

Today, feng shui has a place in modern building design, and feng shui principles have been included in the construction of important new sites, including the Bank of China building in Hong Kong and the Hong Kong and Shanghai Bank.

Temple feng shui

Feng shui occupies a most important part in the building of any Chinese temple. The temple has to be in keeping with the right balance of yin and yang, and it's essential that the temple is sited in exactly the right location, where it will not interfere with the ch'i, and will also fit in with the land, water, wind and so on. It is useful to understand what a building with perfect feng shui is like – you may find some features that you can incorporate into your home.

Good feng shui dictates that a temple be built on *either the pulse of the dragon or in front of a dragon stretching down from hill to sea*. This means that the temple should be built in the valley between two hills and sloping down towards the sea.

Three halls or towers

Both the inside and the outside of the temple have much attention lavished on them. The traditional Chinese temple has three halls. They don't have dividing walls. The front hall is the *bell tower*, where the Taoist priest keeps the temple's bell and drum. In front of the bell tower is the *smoke tower*: here are kept large urns in which are burned the paper offerings – these have wishes and prayers written on them. Finally, behind the smoke tower is the *main palace*. Here is where you find the altar and the images of whichever gods the temple is dedicated to. Sometimes the smoke tower has a ventilator shaft or is open to the sky, much like a courtyard, to help the smoke escape. All the very ancient temples, however, have a roof over the smoke hall, which means that over the centuries the roofs have become blackened with soot. To the sides of the three halls are the *side halls*. Here the priest lives with his family.

Traditional colours

All the old temples are substantial buildings of brick and stone. They are always decorated in the traditional colours believed to bring beneficial effects: red for happiness, green for renewal, black for comfort and nurturing, and white for peace (white is also the colour of mourning among the Chinese). The temples also have elaborate carvings of mythical beasts such as the dragon and phoenix. These animals are often decorated in gold to represent wealth.

Curved roofs

The roofs of the temples are curved to allow the flow of ch'i to be harmonious, and they are usually coloured green. The special porcelain roof tiles are considered an essential part of the fabric of the building and when the temple needs re-roofing they are reverently taken down, eventually to be replaced in exactly the same place as before.

The Dragon's Pearl

On the roof of a Chinese temple there is invariably a large ball – often painted blue. This is known as the *Dragon's Pearl*, or even the *Buddha's Bead*. It is, however, a Taoist symbol and nothing to do with Buddhism. It represents the cosmos – the Taoist's *blue bag*, an affectionate term for the universe.

Dragons and carp

Either side of the Dragon's Pearl you may see a dragon or a carp. These two bring good luck and protect the temple from any evil influences that may be circulating above the roof. The dragon is a benevolent beast of great wisdom and protection. The carp is, of course, a baby dragon – a symbol of success overcoming adversity.

The Flaming Pearl of Wealth

You may often see a small ball in the mouth of carved stone dragons. This is placed there as one of the Taoist's Eight Great Treasures.

Carved lions

The temples often have carvings of lions. This may seem strange as the lion is not indigenous to China; it was introduced by the Buddhists, who arrived from India. The lion was always placed at the entrance to Buddhist temples as a protector, and the Taoists added the lion to their list of protective animals.

Feng shui in the West

Many businesses operating in both the East and West now see the value of feng shui principles being incorporated into building design and décor. They include Citibank, J.P. Morgan, Chase Manhattan and the Asian Wall Street Journal offices.

In the United Kingdom the house building firm Wimpey Homes has issued a 12-page 'beginner's guide to feng shui' for prospective purchasers of new homes. Their feng shui-inspired advice includes injunctions to treat your home as an expression of yourself and to love it as such; to bring nature into your home so that you are never the only living thing in the house; to provide a personal retreat or sanctuary in the home and have a natural gathering place as a communal space. It adds that the colour yellow is a good colour for this space, in a picture, bowl or vase of flowers. Yellow is associated with relaxation and nurturing – it also represents the centre, which is where a communal space should be as it shares all the compass directions. The guide also says that first impressions are important, so keep the outside neat and tidy.

Wimpey Homes is not alone: other companies which practise feng shui principles in their businesses include Marks and Spencer, Virgin Atlantic, the Ritz hotel chain, and the Orange mobile phone network.

When B&Q Warehouse, the home improvements chain, opened its first warehouse in the Far East, in Taiwan, the General Manager, David Inglis, became intrigued: 'at first I thought it was just rather amusing, but when I saw how deeply the Taiwanese believed in it, and how strictly they made feng shui principles a way of life, I began to read more about it and became more deeply interested myself,' he said.

3

putting
feng shui
into
practice

The PahKwa can be divided into eight enrichments, which relate to the main areas of our lives, such as fame, wealth and health. The enrichments can be applied to a house by overlying the PahKwa on its plan, so that the spaces within the house can be related to areas of our lives. If ch'i can be encouraged to flow naturally and at its proper speed through an enrichment, the related aspect of our life will be enhanced. Remedies can be used to speed up ch'i where it is sluggish, or to slow it down where it too violent or vigorous. The remedies, which include light, sound, movement, stillness and colour, can be interpreted in different ways to suit the enrichment and the physical environment of the house.

The feng shui of a house is assessed by a process known as Walking the Nine Palaces, which we will explore at the end of this chapter.

The eight enrichments

Much of Chinese compass feng shui fits the concept of everything being divided into eight areas – eight compass directions, eight seasons, eight types of ch'i, eight types of sha. It also incorporates the eight main areas of our lives – fame, wealth, health, wisdom, friends, family relationships, children and pleasure.

If we refer back to the octagon in Figure 7, we can see that the eight compass directions are each influenced by a particular type of ch'i. Each type of ch'i influences a different area or *enrichment* of our life. These enrichments take into account virtually every facet of life that we need to be able to perform as successful, satisfied adults. If the ch'i from a particular compass direction has become sha then it will adversely affect that area.

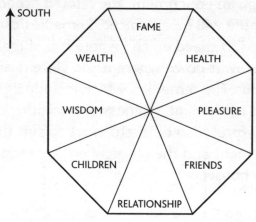

Figure 11 *The eight enrichments.*

The PahKwa

The PahKwa (sometimes spelt *bagua*) with its eight enrichments works for an ideal house – that is, one that faces south.

However, if your house faces east or north, we move the PahKwa round to face that direction. The fame enrichment is always positioned over your front door.

The lo shu magic square

Each of the eight enrichments has a number designated to it, as shown below.

* fame – 1
* wealth – 8
* wisdom and experience – 3
* children and family – 4
* relationship – 9
* friends, new beginnings – 2
* pleasure and indulgence – 7
* health and happiness – 6

If you draw the PahKwa as a square, inserting the number 5 into the middle and the designated numbers in the appropriate part of the grid, the numbers form a *lo shu*, or magic square. (The 5 represents the Jen Hsin, which we will come to later.) Add the numbers in any direction and they add up to 15. The lo shu is an ancient Chinese device used for various ritualistic purposes and its layout is incorporated into many building designs. It is also valuable for *walking the Nine Palaces*, which is a way of checking the feng shui of a building.

8	1	6
3	5	7
4	9	2

Figure 12 *The lo shu magic square.*

We need now to look at these eight enrichments to see how they affect our lives, why the differing ch'i affects them and why they are important to feng shui.

Fame

Fame, or reputation, is the area from which you step out into the world, where you present your 'face' to the rest of the world. Your fame enrichment is influenced by what is immediately visible as you open your front door. What do you see? Hopefully a 'good' view – one that is invigorating, hopeful and inspiring – because this is how you will perceive the world. Open your front door on to 'negative' views such as seedy back streets, factories or rubbish dumps and that will affect your dealings with the outside world. Your emotional horizons are influenced by what is outside your front door – the wider the view the greater your scope for coping with what the world can throw at you. The more limited and narrow the view the more subject to stress and 'loss of face' you will be. The area of your fame enrichment is not only what you can see outside your front door but also what you have immediately inside it. What have you got there?

Traditionally in Western homes this may well be an area where you keep the equipment you need to step out into the world – your overcoat, umbrella, keys, etc. It's also the area where the world comes in to you. How the world perceives you is influenced by how you approach the world.

Ideally, your fame enrichment should have elements of the colour red in it. Red is bright and full of life – fire to motivate you in the world. This is the area of the Red Phoenix, the bird of recovery.

What ch'i comes from the south? Vigorous ch'i – ch'i to make you feel fired up and ready to take on the world, ready to enhance your fame, improve your 'face' and spread your reputation successfully. Vigorous ch'i degrades to accelerating sha. This can cause you to feel exhausted – it all becomes too much for you. Accelerated sha needs to be remedied to make it vigorous ch'i – we will find out how to do this later.

Wealth

Your wealth enrichment is the second most important area, according to traditional Chinese feng shui, and this is the second most auspicious place to have your front door. Your wealth enrichment is where you find your magnet to attract money. Look at the area to the left of your front door (looking from the inside). What have you got there? This is what is affecting your money-earning potential. Is this a good area? Is it full of light and beauty or dark and ugly and unused? How's your bank balance? Beautiful or dark? Your wealth enrichment benefits from creative ch'i – it creates wealth as it arrives so you may need to check what the ch'i is passing before it arrives in your wealth enrichment. Creative ch'i degrades to provoking sha. This can make you irritable – it can also cause you to spend money too freely on things you don't really need or want. If money slips through your fingers faster than water, you need to look closely at this area and see what is causing this. Perhaps there's a small downstairs cloakroom here with a dripping tap or leaking pipes?

Health and happiness

Your health is the enrichment to the right of your front door. Ideally, it will face south-west, ready to benefit from the soothing ch'i that flows from this direction. Soothing ch'i helps your health by easing your stress. It also enables you to find peace and happiness here. This should be an area where you can relax and take time out. Soothing ch'i degrades to disruptive sha. This can cause you to feel angry – and anger is a symptom of stress. How can you relax and enjoy peace and happiness if you're always feeling angry? Check this area carefully and make sure it is comfortable and relaxing.

Wisdom and experience

In Chinese culture the dragon is a symbol of wisdom and benevolence and the Green Dragon lives in the east. What better place to have your wisdom and experience enrichment, where it can benefit from all that dragon energy? Ideally, here you'd have well-rounded green hills – the back of the sleeping dragon – and in the enrichment you'd provide a place to study and keep your scholastic honours. What do you have in your wisdom enrichment?

Your wisdom enrichment benefits from growing ch'i – and you grow in wisdom and experience every day. The dragon is the symbol of spring; each day has the potential to teach you more than you knew yesterday, to grow in stature and maturity. Growing ch'i degrades to overpowering sha which causes us to feel egotistic and vain.

Pleasure and indulgence

Your pleasure enrichment is the area governed by the White Tiger – unpredictable and potentially dangerous. Ideally, to the west of your home you'd have a small lake surrounded by wildflowers to calm the enormous power of the Tiger. Too big a lake and the Tiger will devour you; too small and there will be no excitement in your life. Your pleasure enrichment is the area where you entertain, if that's how you seek your pleasure. It's an ideal place to have your dining room where you can serve delicious meals to your friends and indulge yourself. Changeable ch'i is unpredictable – like the power of the Tiger – and can turn to dangerous sha easily, which can cause us to act rashly – perhaps drink a little too much or take things too easily and become lazy. The blowing wind of changeable ch'i refreshes us and keeps us on our toes but too much and we can feel unsettled; this is what causes the rashness.

Relationship

Traditionally, this enrichment is the area that relates to marriage. However, in the West there is a tendency towards 'relationships' rather than marriage so that is how we will refer to it. Your relationship area should be situated in the north, ideally. Relationships benefit from the nurturing ch'i of the north but if it is allowed to degrade to lingering sha it causes lethargy – and that is the biggest cause of failure in any relationship. If we don't work at it and endeavour to keep it fresh and exciting it will atrophy and die. It makes sense to keep the area of relationship at the back of the house, in the north, to protect our loved ones and keep them safe. This is why your children and family enrichment is also here. Ideally, we'd have the black hills of the Tortoise behind us to protect the most vulnerable members of our family. Your relationship enrichment is traditionally associated with an area of warmth and sleepiness. Here we can have the family fireside and enjoy the nurturing ch'i.

Children and family

This is the area in which to feed young babies, to keep a comfortable chair by the fire to read stories to children, even keep the television if that's what it takes to keep the children entertained. What do you have here? Your children enrichment benefits from flourishing ch'i, and what could be better for growing offspring? However, it degrades to stagnating sha which is a cause of ill health. Check this area carefully if you want your children to flourish. Your children enrichment enjoys both the nurturing power of the Black Tortoise and the wisdom of the Green Dragon and that is probably all that children really need for them to flourish and grow healthily and well. Your children enrichment is probably the most protected area and that is where children need to be, safe and secure nestling between the sleepy hills of the north and the wise hills of the east.

Friends, new beginnings

Your friendship enrichment is the ideal area for sounding out new ideas, new projects. Here you can discuss your plans for the future, prepare for your holidays, chat to friends and get their advice. This is an enrichment where improvements in your life will begin. It benefits from expansive ch'i combining the nurture of the north with the change blowing in from the west. A good place to dream a little, to wish a little, to allow your imagination to take wing and chance all those plans you'd never dared hope for. Your friends will gravitate naturally towards this area when they visit; keep a bottle of good wine here and they will enjoy that expansive ch'i. Limit them a little or you'll find you're sitting up half the night talking new plans and ideas. Watch the expansive ch'i, though, as it degrades to unpredictable sha. If left unremedied, it can cause friends to suddenly stop dropping in, or your plans to come to nothing – or to be altered into something you *didn't* want.

The eight remedies

It seems logical that if there are eight compass directions, eight types of ch'i, eight types of sha and eight enrichments then there will be eight remedies – and there are, of course.

For ch'i to bring you health and good fortune it must be allowed to flow in its natural way – this is in smooth curves and at the proper speed. Too fast and it will cause disruption and allow anger to manifest. Too slow and it will stagnate and cause lethargy and depression. Ch'i likes to flow gently through open spaces and if you provide clutter and untidy areas it will become confused and unfocused. Ch'i likes harmony and beauty, cleanliness and balance.

You should be aware of what the ch'i has flowed through or near before it arrives at your home as it is liable to pick up residues of any unpleasant occurrences. Ch'i dislikes straight lines that cause it to pick up speed and flow too quickly. It also dislikes being trapped in small confined areas. When you *walk the Nine Palaces*, which we will do later in this chapter, you imagine yourself being the ch'i and you can ask yourself if you too could flow smoothly through your home or would you be obstructed, confused, confined, accelerated or stagnated? If you find that the ch'i is not being allowed to flow as freely as it needs to, then you may find it manifests in your life as lack of money, an unfortunate relationship, an inability to relax, loss of friends, noisy and badly behaved children or even, perhaps, ill health. If the ch'i is being impeded in any way you will need one of the eight remedies which are: light, sound, colour, life, movement, stillness, functional objects, straight lines.

Light

This includes lights, mirrors and reflective surfaces. Mirrors are probably the most widely known feng shui remedy. They can be used in most situations. They will reflect bad ch'i, sha, back out of a building, encourage good ch'i to flow in by capturing a pleasant view from outside, lighten and enlarge small dark rooms, deflect ch'i around hidden corners, even change the psychology of a room.

Used in conjunction with lamps, mirrors can transform a room completely. Lights should be as bright as possible without causing glare. You should never be able to see a bare bulb. The Chinese use a lot of lights outside the house and in the garden to fill in missing or dead ch'i. Lights can enhance a dull garden.

Traditionally in China, special octagonal mirrors have been used to deflect unpleasant ch'i back to where it has come from. The mirrors are placed facing outwards towards whatever it was that was regarded as incorrect. If your house faces a graveyard or factory, a small mirror placed to reflect the sha will improve the ch'i entering your home. Any dark areas or corners of your home can be livened up by placing good-quality lamps in them. Soft lighting is best to create harmony. You can also use mirrors to encourage light into darker areas or placed at the end of long corridors to slow the ch'i down. Light remedies are traditionally associated with your *fame* enrichment.

Sound

Most people associate Chinese culture with wind chimes without realizing that they are an important feng shui remedy. Anything that makes sound can also be used: bells, metal mobiles, bamboo tubes, etc. Melodic noises can help to break up stagnant ch'i by causing swirls and eddies of sound in the air. Wind chimes also act as gentle alarms to tell us when someone has entered our house. Pleasing and harmonious sounds are also good attractants of lucky ch'i: they are said to encourage wealth into buildings. The sound of water flowing is beneficial. Fountains can be seen as both movement and sound.

Harsh noises cause ch'i to become jangled and unharmonious. You can use wind chimes, bells, even the sound of water fountains to create a harmony of sound and soothe the ch'i. Sound remedies are traditionally associated with your *friends* enrichment, so you can play music here to provide your guests with harmonious sound.

Colour

The Chinese are great believers in using colour to stimulate the flow of ch'i, especially the four dominant colours of red, white, gold/green and black. These are lucky colours associated with attracting fame, activity, wisdom and wealth. In the West more subtle colour schemes are generally preferred, but it is useful to remember that a sudden patch of bright, strong colour in a stagnating room can stimulate ch'i effectively.

Any area where you feel stressed or irritable should be decorated simply in pale colours, white is best, and then a single, simple flash of bright colour introduced to focus the ch'i and keep it vibrant. Colour is traditionally associated with your *children* enrichment since it stimulates them.

Life

Plants are mainly used to fill in blank areas where there isn't any ch'i or to help ch'i that is stagnating to 'come to life' again. They can be used to hide disruptive, sharp corners that poke into rooms and stimulate ch'i in areas where it might linger. Large plants can be used to slow ch'i down when it is being directed too quickly along straight lines. Fish in aquariums are also used for the same purpose. The Chinese for 'fish' and for 'money' is the same word so they often use fish to represent wealth. That's why you will often see fish tanks next to the cash register in Chinese restaurants – it encourages you to spend freely.

When ch'i is weakening or causing a depletion of energy or life force you need to introduce some element of life into an area. Pot plants are best but they should have rounded leaves. Cut flowers aren't a good idea as their ch'i is leaking away as they die, and dried flowers are frowned on as they have no life left in them. Plants should not be left untended or allowed to get dusty. Traditionally, plants are associated with your *wealth* enrichment. The Chinese use fish in tanks to introduce life into an area. If you want to do the same you should keep an odd number of fish: goldfish are recommended.

Movement

Where ch'i needs to be stimulated or deflected, use a moving object. The Chinese use flags, silk banners, ribbons, fountains, wind chimes, mobiles and weather vanes. Moving objects should use the natural power of the wind if possible and be made of natural materials.

The smoke from incense can be regarded as movement and be used beneficially but obviously only short term.

Flowing water brings ch'i to the building but it should move gently and gurgle rather than roar. An ideal location for a house is one where it faces south with a babbling brook in the south east bringing in lots of money.

Movement is associated with your *relationship* enrichment and this is where we need movement to stop things getting stale and being taken for granted.

Stillness

Any large inanimate object such as a statue or large rock can bring stillness to an otherwise too-fast ch'i area. This is especially beneficial in gardens where the path to a front gate can cause the ch'i to leave too quickly. A statue should blend harmoniously into your home and have a particular significance for you. You can use large natural objects like driftwood or a bleached, gnarled branch.

In China, there is an area in the home where a statue is placed to provide a focus for spirituality. This is often a Buddha but you could use any large, beautiful object. It should be simple but exquisite and it will slow ch'i down and help to purify it. Traditionally associated with your *pleasure* enrichment, a still object will allow you many happy hours relaxing and contemplating natural beauty or the perfection of a craftsperson's labour.

Functional objects

In traditional feng shui, this usually meant machinery or tools but nowadays it can be extended to include any electrical equipment used in the home: televisions, stereos, electrical fans and, probably most important of all, computers. Electricity and ch'i need to be harmoniously regarded if they are not to clash: both need to be treated with respect. Electrical equipment can stimulate ch'i but sometimes it can overstimulate it, so keep it to a minimum.

Anything functional or manufactured that does a job of work, or is a tool, can be used to stir up dull ch'i – anything from a refrigerator to an electric kettle. You need to be careful not to overdo it as functional devices tend to be strong remedies. Traditionally, functional objects are associated with your *wisdom and experience* enrichment so this is a perfect place to keep your computer.

Straight lines

The Chinese use flutes, swords, scrolls, bamboo tubes and fans to break up ch'i when it moves heavily or sluggishly, especially along beams and long corridors. The straight lines are hung at an angle to create the PahKwa octagonal shape and that helps to direct the ch'i away from the beam or corridor and back into the rooms.

Although we have talked of ch'i disliking straight lines, there are times when ch'i needs to be enlivened or interrupted. Perhaps you have beams that ch'i can flow along too quickly; you can use anything that has straight lines in it such as the items described above to break up the ch'i and deflect it into the room. Straight lines are traditionally associated with your *health* enrichment.

Using remedies

Here are some tips on how to recognize when you need to apply a remedy. Check each of the eight areas of your life. How are your finances? Your relationship? Your health? Your fame and reputation? Check each one in turn. If you are happy with that particular area of your life, you don't need a remedy there. But if you are experiencing problems, you may need to do some work on that area. Let's suppose it's your finances that are suffering. You check the area and find that your money enrichment falls in your dining room. Perhaps you've been eating all your money? If you visit a Chinese restaurant you may see, as we said earlier, a fish tank near the cash register – this is to encourage money to come to life. Perhaps you could try placing a fish tank in your dining room? Or a large plant to encourage the ch'i to provide good fortune?

Suppose it's your relationship area that is suffering and you check that enrichment area to find that it falls in your study. Perhaps you have been devoting too much time to work? You could try introducing a wind chime above your desk to stir the ch'i up, or how about one of those executive desk toys that moves? Or if you have your computer here, try running a moving 'screen saver' when you're not using it.

What ch'i likes and dislikes

Remember that ch'i likes: harmony, gentle curves, beauty, spaciousness, order. Ch'i dislikes: disorder, clutter, straight lines, neglected areas.

Sometimes you have to completely revamp your house – not because the decoration is wrong but because decay and neglect have set in. Ch'i likes spring cleaning and freshness. Sometimes that's all you need to do to an area to benefit from better ch'i – tidy up and spring clean.

Remedies and their ideal enrichments

Each of the eight remedies has a particular enrichment area in which it works best:
* light – associated with your *fame* enrichment
* sound – associated with your *friends* enrichment
* colour – associated with your *children* enrichment
* life – associated with your *money* enrichment
* movement – associated with your *relationship* enrichment
* stillness – associated with your *pleasure* enrichment
* functional objects – associated with your *education* enrichment
* straight lines – associated with your *health* enrichment.
Those are the basic principles upon which feng shui is based.

Which way does your house face?

There are eight different directions in which your house can face. Remember the direction is set by the direction of your front door. You may use a side entrance, climb in through a window, swing down from the roof – and it won't make a bit of difference.

The house direction is set by the front door direction. If you choose to use another entrance then that says something significant about you and your dwelling; this is one aspect you should look at carefully. Perhaps if you use a different entrance – such as a side entrance – you may be seeking a different enrichment as the dominant one, or a different ch'i to work with, or even a different element type to live with.

Yin and yang

Before we look at the different house directions, we need to understand more about yin and yang. There are four yang directions and four yin directions.

The four yang directions
* east
* south-east
* south
* south-west.

In the ideal south-facing house, these correspond to four enrichments:
* wisdom and experience
* wealth
* fame
* health and happiness.

These are known as the *four personal enrichments*. These are all yang, all corresponding with the 'male' principle; the 'I' part of life. They are concerned with the individual; your own personal wisdom, wealth, fame and health.

The four yin directions
* west
* north-west
* north
* north-east.

In the south-facing house, these correspond to the four yin enrichments:

* pleasure and indulgence
* friends and new beginnings
* relationship
* children and family.

They are known as the *four collective enrichments* and correspond with the yin or 'female' principle. They are all to do with 'us'.

You may have noticed the four yang personal enrichments are all located at the front of the house whereas the four yin collective enrichments are located at the back of the house.

The front of a house is yang – personal, confident, bold, outward.

The back of a house is *yin* – collective, nurturing, protective, inward.

Walking the Nine Palaces

In China when a house was first built no one would live in it until the local Taoist priest had blessed it. The priest would probably have been instrumental in helping with the design of the house anyway. The priest would *walk the Nine Palaces*. This entails walking through the house according to a ritual which is based on the *lo shu*, the magic square (see Figure 12). You should always use this ritualistic way of walking through your home whenever you need to check any of the enrichments.

Walking the Nine Palaces mentally fixes what you are actually doing. This isn't a casual stroll through your home wondering if you need to redecorate. You are following an ancient way and those who have gone before you would appreciate your time and respect in continuing the tradition.

Taking your time

In the West we tend to rush at things too much. Walking the Nine Palaces is an Eastern philosophy and one that goes on at a slower pace. If you rush through walking the Nine Palaces you may miss that tiny detail that will change things for you. If you rush this walk, you don't allow your home the space to speak to you, to tell you what it feels is wrong and what it would like corrected. Feng shui is not an exact science, it can't be proved by reason or logic. It functions on a different level from anything else we encounter and we need to open channels into our intuitive nature. The Taoist priests knew this and when they walked the Nine Palaces with the house's new owner they would take their time, stopping in each enrichment to allow the owner and the house to get acquainted, to become one with each other. In each enrichment they would have lit some incense and burned paper prayers — these were written in traditional Chinese calligraphy on rice paper and they flare up quickly, the burned embers rising upwards taking the prayer heavenwards.

Your living home

In the West, many people feel that a home is just somewhere to rest for a while before going back to work. In China, a home is seen as a living being. It needs breath and life for it to enrich us and protect us properly. If we neglect our relationship with our home then we will be much poorer in spirit. Feng shui is about relearning things we may have forgotten. The fabric of the building is as important as the decor; the decor as important as the furnishings; the furnishings as important as the light, air and breath of the house. All of these are as important as us, the living occupants of the house.

The nine questions

Back to the Nine Palaces. You start at your front door, which we will call **1**. At each enrichment, stop and listen. As you are walking the Nine Palaces you need to ask nine questions in each enrichment.

* How does this area feel to you?
* How do you feel about it?
* What would you change in this enrichment?
* What feels right here?

* What feels wrong?
* What problems have you encountered in your life that relate to this enrichment?
* What can you take away from this area?
* What is missing from this area?
* If you were starting from scratch, would you have this area the same as it is now?

Your front door is **1** – your fame area. Open your front door, look out and ask the nine questions. When, and only when, you are satisfied with the answers, move on to the next area. Imagine that Taoist priest is standing with you and asking the questions. What answers would you give? Perhaps you might like to do this exercise with someone you really trust, someone whose advice and guidance you respect. Get them to ask you the nine questions. Your answers may sound different if you have to say them out loud. It's as if having to justify the answers to another person has the capacity to make us really sure of what we feel and say about a particular area.

Once you have finished with your assessment of your fame enrichment, then you can move on to **2** – friends and new beginnings. You will find this area immediately to the right at the back of your home – the back right-hand corner – assuming, as we will for all these directions, that you are facing the front door. Once you have asked everything here you can move on. Sometimes walking the Nine Palaces can take some time. You should allow at least a whole day for this – you inevitably get side-tracked, caught up in examining the tiniest detail of not only how and where you live but also why and what for. The nine questions may spark off all sorts of unexpected lines of enquiry – so take your time, this is not to be rushed.

Move on to **3** – your wisdom and experience enrichment. You will find this along the left-hand side of your home. Again, ask the questions, and when you are ready move on to **4** – children and family. You will find this immediately behind your wisdom enrichment. These two enrichments are connected, they flow into each other. Remember that your *children* may not be your physical offspring, although your children enrichment is usually taken to mean just that. In this area you should again ask the nine questions and be satisfied with the answers before you move on to **5** – the centre of your home.

Jen Hsin – the centre

This is not an enrichment but it is known as *Jen Hsin* – which can only really be translated as *heart of the heart*. This is the very centre of your home, and it deserves special consideration. If you are not sure exactly where the centre of your home lies, then it may be worth measuring it. You can pace out two diagonal lines between the four corners of your home and the point where they intersect will be Jen Hsin. Once you've found it you have only to see what you've got there to recognize what your home revolves around. This is the pivot, and your home, possibly your life, revolves around this heart centre. If you are unhappy about what you have here, or you feel that this is not the right thing for your home to rotate around, then change it. Replace whatever you have here with something more suitable. This is quite a surprising exercise to do and you may be in for a shock when you discover what it is that forms the heart centre of your home.

Continuing the nine questions

Once you have finished here you move on to **6** – your health, peace and happiness enrichment. You will find this area to the right of the front of your home – the right-hand corner, if you like. Again, ask the nine questions and, when you are ready, you can move on to **7** – pleasure and indulgence. This area is the right-hand side of your home, directly behind your health enrichment. While you are checking out your pleasure and indulgence enrichment you can sit down here and see if this area really is as comfortable as it ought to be.

Now move on to **8** – your wealth enrichment. This is the left-hand corner of your home. Again, ask the nine questions and when you are ready move on to **9** – relationship. This is the back of your home, nestling between children and friends. Perhaps here you should be asking the questions with your partner.

Once you have finished with 9 – relationship, you should go back to 1 – fame. Here you should again check everything is in order. During the walking of the Nine Palaces you may have changed many things and you need to check that the first area is still in harmony, in balance, with all the changes you have made.

From yang to yin, from yin to yang

You may have noticed that as you walk the Nine Palaces you are constantly crossing from a yang area to a yin area, and back to a yang area. As you move between yin and yang, yang and yin, see how the mood of each area changes. Yin areas should be as light and bright as possible; yang areas can be darker and quieter. The principle of yin and yang is that they always seek the opposite – so you can provide it by knowing which each wants to be in harmony.

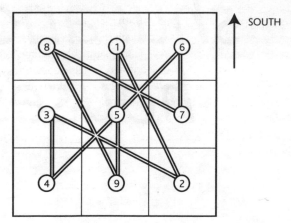

SOUTH

Figure 13 *The eight-pointed star.*

You may also have noticed the shape of the ground plan you are tracing as you walk the Nine Palaces. This strange eight-pointed star shape (see Figure 13) is designed so that you cross and recross each area the same number of times and so that you always move between yin and yang.

4

feng shui and houses

The location of a house and the direction in which it faces affect the energy flows around and through the house. Key aspects of the location are mountains (or tall buildings) near the house and the buildings in the immediate neighbourhood; water – whether running streams or still lakes or ponds; trees – whose yin will balance the yang of buildings; and the actual house structure.

The house direction can be any one of the eight points of the compass, and each brings a different combination of enrichments and ch'i energies. For example, in the ideal south-facing house, the fame enrichment may benefit from the vigorous ch'i of the south (or suffer from the south's accelerating sha), but if the house faces south-east, the fame enrichment would be aligned with the creative ch'i of the south-east. The ch'i and enrichment combinations for each direction of house are covered in this chapter.

Making the home pleasant and harmonious

As we spend most of our time at home it makes sense to ensure that it is as pleasant and harmonious as possible. In the West, decor and interior design are used for that, while in China feng shui is used as well. The Chinese are as concerned as Westerners to ensure that the visual impression is pleasing but they also like to make sure that the energy flow in and around the home is as beneficial as possible.

We need to check a few key areas when we apply feng shui to our homes. If we work through them in order it will make it easier for you to remember when you come to apply the principles to your own home.

Mountains and surroundings

If you do not live near mountains, the principles of feng shui can still apply if you consider any tall buildings near you as 'mountains'. Their towering presence can overpower your ch'i. Concave and convex mirrors can turn their image upside down, which will negate the effect of their powerful ch'i. Similarly, the reflection from a bowl of water will have the effect of flattening their image.

Any tall buildings should, ideally, be in the Tortoise and Dragon areas – to the north and east. If they are not, you will have to flatten them – with mirrors, of course – to make flat zones in your Phoenix and Tiger areas, to the south and west. Place small mirrors in the window facing outwards.

'Surroundings' means checking the immediately surrounding neighbourhood for good or bad feng shui. What are the neighbours like? Are there ugly buildings close to you? You need to look out from the eight cardinal points of your home to see what is there. You also need to check the eight types of ch'i that may be directed at your home.

Start by physically standing outside your home in each of the eight cardinal compass points and look to see what is there.

For example, you may stand with your back to the side of the house that faces south and find yourself looking at a particularly unpleasant factory. Is this really where you want your vigorous yang ch'i to come from? What about the side of the house facing the factory? Is it your main entrance or a blank wall? If it is blank then the factory ch'i will not do too much damage but what if it is your front door? What if the factory makes armaments or weapons of some sort, or uses dangerous chemicals? What sort of effect do you think *that* ch'i would have on you and your life?

East

Stand and look east from where the growing ch'i is coming. This ch'i stimulates you, gives you your creative energy. So what's there? Another factory? A splendid view of rolling hills? Which would you prefer?

North

Look to the north, the direction of nurturing ch'i. This is the sleepy stuff that you can roll up in and hibernate. Ideally, it should undulate down from the Tortoise hills in a gentle embracing way. What have you got there?

West

To the west is the changeable ch'i. It is disruptive and unpredictable. The Chinese sometimes say it is dangerous and destructive. Where's your west ch'i coming from? How is it getting into the house? Is this your main entrance or a back door that you hardly ever use? If it is the main entrance you need to deflect it firmly. Use the largest mirror you can on the inside wall immediately opposite the door so that the sha is deflected straight back out again. If it is a back door you can use a smaller mirror or wind chimes to break up the sha as it enters. If you don't use the door too much then it's not so imperative to deflect the sha. What windows open on to the west? Have a look and decide how much sha can get in through them. You can deflect sha by hanging small balls of glass in the window to spin round on thread and give off prisms of colour as they catch the light.

The Chinese traditionally used to black out any west-facing windows.

South-east

This is where your creative ch'i is coming from. What's there to stimulate your creative processes?

South-west

Soothing ch'i comes from the south-west. But is it soothing? It will pick up a lot from whatever it passes through or over just before it arrives at your home.

North-east

Flourishing ch'i comes to us from the north-east.

North-west

This is the home of expansive ch'i, but if it has passed over or through anything unpleasant it can cause us to feel extremely unsettled when it reaches us.

Joined houses and flats

Obviously, if you live in a semi-detached or terraced house you can't do this test on all walls.

If you live in a terrace, the ch'i coming from your neighbours is important. You can also go to each end of the terrace to see what is coming towards the whole line of houses.

If you live in a block of flats or high-rise building, you have the added complication of what is coming up from below. Maybe you live above a shop. What sort of shop? What sort of ch'i is filtering up through your floors? The Chinese would never live above a funeral director's but might be very happy to live above a bank.

Living in a basement, a very yin place, needs consideration as to what is above you. Again it may be shops or other flats. The Chinese feel that any place that may have been subject to emotional distress, like a police station, a prison, army barracks or hospital, gives off a particular type of ch'i called *fan ch'i*, translated as *offensive ch'i* and it can be harmful, causing you to feel the same emotional distress as was originally generated.

Feng shui and harmony

A lot of feng shui is intuitive work. We can't give examples of every type of house and the direction it could face. You have to look yourself and feel whether the energy is right. A lot of feng shui is also common sense. If, every time you open your front door, you are confronted with a dreadful view you are bound to feel worse than if you look out on a wonderful vista of countryside, streams and beautiful hills. Your quality of life improves with the quality of your horizons. You might think you can't control your view – but you can. You can usually choose where you live and when to move or what to do to remedy anything wrong. Feng shui is about taking responsibility; feng shui is about waking up to choice. You can improve your surroundings but ultimately you may have to move if you come to realize that where and how you live is adversely affecting your emotional and spiritual horizons.

Water and wind

We need water around us. If we haven't the privilege of living near a river or stream then we have to add the water ourselves. That's why aquariums are so important to the Chinese.

Water carries ch'i as well as being a soothing element of our environment. If there are rivers and streams near us we need to look at the way they will bring ch'i to us. Using the principles that we have already learned we can work out which are good and which are bad. Ch'i, which is beneficial, likes to meander; sha, which is disruptive, likes to travel in straight lines. So, does the river head straight for your home or wander happily around it? Is it a gently babbling brook or a concrete-banked canal? Guess which carries ch'i and which carries sha. It's time for you to do some work now.

Do you look out over a lake? Large bodies of water such as lakes, reservoirs, even large ponds, accumulate ch'i. Is it overwhelming? Even worse, is it in the west? A lake here would store sha in large quantities and would almost certainly be an extraordinarily powerful force that would erupt unpredictably. Is the lake in the north? This could make you very sleepy.

We need water in the home and if we can use mirrors to reflect watery views inside, so much the better. The sight and sound of water moving naturally can be most beneficial and soothing.

Trees

The Chinese word for trees in a feng shui context is *liu*, which is directly translated as 'willow'. The willow is the tree most often represented in traditional Chinese landscape paintings (which are called *shan-shui*). If we see buildings as the yang element of the landscape then trees are the yin: and we need both for our spirit to be nurtured. The shan-shui painters work on a ratio of 3 to 2: three yang elements to two yin. They also see, as do feng shui practitioners, hills as yang and hollows as yin. If you take a panorama, three-fifths should be yang, the sky, and two-fifths yin, the landscape. We can use yin trees to balance an excess of yang buildings or yang hills. In the West this ratio is also used and is known as the 'golden section', a proportion as important in Western art as it is in Eastern. *Liu* can also be understood as 'garden'.

Dwelling

This is the feng shui of the actual building itself: the walls, the windows, the doors, the rooms and the decor. We will look at this in greater detail in Chapter 5.

Ourselves

There is little point in getting the feng shui right if the heart of the home also needs work doing on it. We can see ourselves as the heart – the *jenhsin*. We need to be as in balance as our home. Getting the feng shui right can make quite a difference but we also need to sort out our own personal feng shui. We are the recipients of all that good ch'i. We have to put ourselves in a position to make good use of it all. Correcting the feng shui and leaving ourselves out of the equation is pointless. The original feng shui practitioners were also Taoist priests. As well as correcting the feng shui of the dwelling they offered advice to the home owner on health and spiritual matters. They corrected any faults with *jenhsin* as they went along.

The eight types of house

As we move the PahKwa round to face the compass direction your house faces, it will be apparent that there are eight basic house directions. Each of these has eight enrichment locations – and consequently benefits from the eight types of ch'i in different ways. For instance, if you have a north-facing house your fame enrichment will not face south but north. The north brings nurturing ch'i. How do you think that will change your reputation or career? Obviously, it will have an effect – and may direct you to working in a more caring profession such as counselling or medicine. Your wisdom enrichment would be in the west – subject to that changeable Tiger ch'i. How would this affect your learning powers? The west is an unpredictable area where we cannot anticipate or plan because we are always subject to the vagaries of fate. Perhaps if you have a north-facing home your wisdom becomes erratic or subject to fits and starts.

Suppose you had a south-west facing home, and you were concerned about your health. Look where your health enrichment falls – in the west again. This could cause your health to be unpredictable – unless you remedy it.

The south-facing house

This is a very yang home – vigorous, creative – out in the world full of energy and light.

1 **South – fame enrichment.** Your fame benefits from vigorous ch'i but can suffer from accelerating sha. This is an area that benefits from lots of light – this shines on your fame like a spotlight – or the flash of a camera.

2 **South-east – wealth enrichment.** Your wealth benefits from creative ch'i but can deteriorate into provoking sha. As you have a south-facing house you probably work in the public eye, perhaps in some creative field?

3 **East – wisdom and experience enrichment.** This is enjoying growing ch'i and should continue to do so unless it degrades to overpowering sha. This area needs a serious functional object to enhance all that wisdom and help you gain experience.

4 **North-east – children and family enrichment.** Here you can enjoy flourishing ch'i. A good place for you to be but how sure are you that you can cope with the noise? This is the area of the thunder; it's arousing and colourful but if neglected the ch'i becomes stagnating sha.

5 **North – relationship enrichment.** This is where your relationship is supposed to be – quiet and sustaining, in the north area of your home and life. The ch'i here is nurturing and you can be enveloped in warmth, love and comfort. If you neglect this area, the ch'i becomes lingering sha which can make you question everything too much.

6 **North-west – friends and new beginnings enrichment.** This is an area enjoying expansive ch'i, but the ch'i can become unpredictable sha. You need to incorporate the stillness of the mountain that symbolizes the north-west into this area. You also need to fill this area with sound to harmonize the sha.

7 **West – pleasure enrichment.** The ch'i here is changeable and needs to be calmed and balanced with a stillness remedy.

8 **South-west – health and happiness enrichment.** The ch'i here is soothing and needs to be encouraged with straight lines. This area is gentle like a soft breeze and can bring you great peace and good health.

The south-east facing house

This is the home of the entrepreneur and the business person. It's a very yang house, full of being out in the world – and the front door opens straight out into the wealth enrichment – good for making money.

1 **South-east – fame enrichment.** Here you step out of your front door straight into the wealth and possessions area of life. This is your area. Here you are happy. What could be better than enjoying all that creative ch'i and using it to make yourself richer and your family better off? However, creative ch'i can become provoking sha. You should settle

this area, if it has become problematic in any way, by using a combination of life and light.

2 **East – wealth enrichment.** Your wealth will come from what you already know – this is a wealth enrichment in the east which is your experience. The ch'i here is growing. The ch'i here can become overpowering – fill this area with life and functional tools.

3 **North-east – wisdom and experience enrichment.** Here you have a yang enrichment benefiting from yin flourishing ch'i. The ch'i can become stagnating sha which can stop any further growth in your wisdom enrichment. You need to combine both colour and a functional object in this area.

4 **North – children and family enrichment.** A good yin enrichment in almost its ideal location. Here the ch'i is nurturing which makes you protective towards your family. However, the ch'i can become lingering sha which could make you overprotective. To counteract this you should incorporate both movement and colour.

5 **North-west – relationship enrichment.** This is a yin enrichment in the yin compass direction of north-west – which is traditionally associated more with friendship than with marriage. The ch'i here is expansive.

6 **West – friends and new beginnings enrichment.** The ch'i here is changeable which can cause your friendships to come and go without warning. Remedy this area with both sound and stillness.

7 **South-west – pleasure enrichment.** A good yin enrichment facing the best yang direction it could – the ch'i here is soothing which couldn't be better for relaxing and indulging yourself.

8 **South – health and happiness enrichment.** If you don't feel healthy with this yang enrichment in such a vigorous yang compass direction then perhaps you are suffering from accelerating sha. Try remedying this with a combination of straight lines and light.

The east-facing house

This is a yang house of someone who likes being out in the world but only to explore, to find out how the world works rather than to take from it.

1 **East – fame enrichment.** When you step out of your front door into your fame area it is into the east, the traditional home of the benevolent Dragon who guides and offers great wisdom. Your reputation may well be, as is the ch'i from the east, growing. Caution should be exercised lest it becomes overpowering sha. Fill this area with light and functional objects.

2 **North-east – wealth enrichment.** Here a typically yang enrichment enters a yin compass direction. The ch'i here is flourishing which means an accumulating wealth enrichment. The ch'i can become stagnating sha if the learning is not being passed on to enough people.

3 **North – wisdom and experience enrichment.** Here your wisdom enrichment is in the north and needs assistance from your partner. This is a good balance of a yang enrichment in a yin compass direction.

4 **North-west – children and family enrichment.** If you want your parenting to be relaxed and happy then you couldn't choose a better direction to be in. The ch'i here could become unpredictable if left unattended. Make sure this area has lots of sound and colour.

5 **West – relationship enrichment.** A yin enrichment in a yin compass direction ought to provide you with good beneficial ch'i but it is changeable – coming from the White Tiger. It can quickly become unpredictable – and extremely volatile. Fill this area with stillness and movement in equal quantities.

6 **South-west – friends and new beginnings enrichment.** The south-west brings soothing, gentle ch'i which will help your friends bring you great peace of mind. The ch'i can become disruptive sha unless remedied.

7 **South – pleasure and indulgence enrichment.** The ch'i can become accelerating here which can exhaust you. Deflect

it with stillness and light – or at least turn it aside before it
totally drains you.

8 **South-east – health and happiness enrichment.** This is
a good yang enrichment in a good yang location. Here your
health is benefiting from creative ch'i and should bring
you joy.

The south-west facing house

This is the house of someone who uses their caring, nurturing
side to help others.

1 **South-west – fame enrichment.** This is the most yin of the
four yang directions. When you step out into the world you
step out into the soothing wind of the south-west and you
find your fame helping others to overcome their difficulties
which will probably be associated with their health – and that
can be physical, emotional or even spiritual.

2 **South – wealth enrichment.** The south is known as the
creative heaven direction, full of invigorating ch'i. If the ch'i
shows any tendency to become accelerating sha – and you
can tell if it has become so from the amount of clutter you
keep in this area – then remedy it with life and light.

3 **South-east – wisdom and experience enrichment.** This is
a good yang enrichment in a good yang compass direction.
Here your wisdom can benefit from creative ch'i. If the ch'i
becomes provoking sha you will have to fill this area with
plants and a functional object.

4 **East – children and family enrichment.** This is a yin
enrichment in a yang compass direction – the balance,
however, is good with your family benefiting from growing
ch'i from the benevolent wisdom of the Dragon. The ch'i can
become overpowering – fill this area with bright, colourful,
functional objects.

5 **North-east – relationship enrichment.** Here your
relationship is benefiting from flourishing ch'i which can be
arousing, but the ch'i can stagnate very easily. All you have to
do is stir it up with lots of colour and movement.

6 **North – friends and new beginnings enrichment.** Here your friendships benefit from nurturing ch'i. Any friendships forged here will last a long time. This is a good yin enrichment in the best yin compass direction for protection and caring. If the ch'i becomes lingering you can help it along with movement and sound.

7 **North-west – pleasure and indulgence enrichment.** Here your pleasure enjoys expansive ch'i. What a good place to relax in and enjoy being you. If the ch'i becomes unpredictable sha you can make it more harmonious by using sound and stillness.

8 **West – health and happiness enrichment.** Here the ch'i is changeable and needs to be watched carefully. This is a yang enrichment in a volatile yin compass direction. The power of the Tiger can be unleashed suddenly and unpredictably and become dangerous sha all too easily. This area needs straight lines which run at right angles away from the west (i.e. north to south) as well as stillness.

The north-facing house

What a good place to have your fame enrichment – your loved ones must know you to be the most caring, sensitive and considerate person there is.

1 **North – fame enrichment.** This is where you are in the world – stepping out with your loved one on your arm. Don't you just feel that everything is right with the world when you are in love? This is the most yang of enrichments in the most yin of compass directions. If the ch'i becomes lingering sha, remedy this by filling this area with movement and light.

2 **North-west – wealth enrichment.** Your finances may grow and shrink with alarming regularity. Settle this area with life and sound.

3 **West – wisdom and experience enrichment.** A yang enrichment in a changeable yin compass direction. If you want to settle the sha here then use a functional object combined with a stillness remedy.

4 **South-west – children and family enrichment.** This is
   an area of angels and beasts. One minute everything is
   perfect and the next it's the end of the world. To pull the
   two extremes towards each other you could use straight
   lines and colour in this area.

5 **South – relationship enrichment.** The most yin enrichment
   in the most yang location. Here's the place for a creative,
   vigorous relationship indeed. If the ch'i becomes accelerating
   sha, remedy this excess of energy with lots of light and
   movement.

6 **South-east – friends and family enrichment.** Your friendships
   enjoy the creative ch'i from this compass direction – they'll
   always find new ways of cheering you up when your love has
   left you. Remedy this area with life and sound.

7 **East – pleasure and indulgence enrichment.** Some people
   like to switch off when they relax and do nothing – but not
   you. However, if you find it difficult to completely unwind then
   use this area to contemplate on a beautiful practical object.

8 **North-east – health and happiness enrichment.** If you
   can balance this yang enrichment with the yin flourishing
   ch'i you can enjoy only good health. However, the ch'i can
   stagnate and you may find yourself depressed by it. Remedy
   it with colour and straight lines.

The north-east facing house

This is known in Chinese feng shui as the Dragon's lair house.
The home of the Dragon indeed, and dragons can't help but give
advice – it's what they're there for.

1 **North-east – fame enrichment.** This is the enrichment
   where you step out into the world – and your world is
   populated with lots of people seeking advice, help, leadership,
   and your time and attention. If the ch'i here stagnates too
   much you may actually be doing nothing. Enliven it with light
   and colour.

2 **North – wealth enrichment.** One of your great dislikes is
   listening to advice from others. Fill this area with life and

movement if you want the lingering sha to return to being nurturing.

3 **North-west – wisdom and experience enrichment.** Keep it simple. Keep it accurate and don't try to teach anyone anything unless they ask. Keep this area from becoming unpredictable by using sound and functional objects.

4 **West – children and family enrichment.** Children like provoking the Dragon and making it roar, and what better place to do it than in the opposite location for it to feel any peace. Remedy this area with colour and stillness.

5 **South-west – relationship enrichment.** Here you can be soothed by all that south-west ch'i. This is a good yin enrichment in a gentle yang location. Your relationship may well benefit from being a work partnership as well. If the ch'i becomes disruptive sha, remedy it and provide yourself with a more peaceful relationship by adding movement and straight lines.

6 **South – friends and new beginnings enrichment.** What a good place to have your friends enrichment. It's a good yin enrichment in a very positive yang location. If anyone tries to hurry you too much then the ch'i has become accelerating sha and you'll need to slow it down by using light remedies and sound remedies.

7 **South-east – pleasure and indulgence enrichment.** This is the place where you should relax and unwind. What have you got here? Is this area benefiting from all that creative ch'i? Or is it being wasted? Is this an area that provokes you? Or that won't let you rest here? Then remedy it with lots of plants and beautiful statues.

8 **East – health and happiness enrichment.** The ch'i here is growing – and it comes from the east, the spring. This is excellent for your health. You can recover quickly, improve your stamina and maintain good all-round health here. If the ch'i becomes overpowering sha you may be tempted to take on too much and exhaust yourself. Remedy this by incorporating a functional object with lots of straight lines into this area.

The north-west facing house

This is the house of someone who looks out for others – care workers and police officers favour the north-west facing home.

1. **North-west – fame enrichment.** When you step out of your front door you step into the north-west. This is all to do with looking after other people. If the ch'i becomes unpredictable sha and you find yourself getting irritable, then remedy this area with light and sound.

2. **West – wealth enrichment.** Your finances, facing in this direction, must be so changeable you wonder if you'll ever be straight money wise. If your finances ever look like becoming a severe problem, then the ch'i has become dangerous sha and you'll need to fill this area with lots of life.

3. **South-west – wisdom and experience enrichment.** You can learn from your mistakes – unlike some other people. If the ch'i becomes disruptive sha then remedy this area with straight lines and functional objects.

4. **South – children and family enrichment.** This is a perfect place for a parent to be. You have limitless energy and great skill at entertaining small people. You delight in small children. If the vigorous ch'i becomes accelerating sha you may find yourself exhausted, so remedy it with lots of colour and light in this area.

5. **South-east – relationship enrichment.** A good yin enrichment that benefits from the creative ch'i of a yang location. If your relationship becomes provoking then remedy this area with lots of plants and lots of movement.

6. **East – friends and new beginnings enrichment.** It doesn't take you long to bounce back from adversity, nor does it take you long to make new friends and settle into new situations. If the ch'i becomes overpowering, remedy this area with functional objects and sound.

7. **North-east – pleasure and indulgence enrichment.** Here you can relax in warmth and comfort. A good yin enrichment in a good yin location. The ch'i here is flourishing and you

should be able to relax easily. If the ch'i becomes stagnating sha, remedy it with lots of colour and stillness.

8 **North – health and happiness enrichment.** You may be prone to injury – only because you rush at everything so eagerly. This enrichment is a good place to recuperate; it's quiet with yin, nurturing ch'i to heal and help you. If the ch'i has become lingering sha you will need to remedy it with movement and straight lines.

The west-facing house

This is the house of the greatest pleasure lovers – and all to do with food.

1 **West – fame enrichment.** As you step out of your front door you step into the great pleasure areas of life. This is the location of changeable ch'i, which means you like variety. You enjoy all the pleasure that this world can offer but if the ch'i becomes dangerous sha the pleasure will turn to overindulgence. If that happens fill this area with light and stillness.

2 **South-west – wealth enrichment.** Too much wealth would unsettle you despite what you think. This south-west wealth enrichment will bring you enough but not too much. The ch'i here soothes rather than inflates. Should it degrade to sha it will be disruptive and you may find your finances cause you more problems than you anticipate. Remedy this area with lots of life and straight lines.

3 **South – wisdom and experience enrichment.** Your wisdom enrichment is in the south which is the most yang of yang locations. This is where we get the most vigorous ch'i from and it can overwhelm us if we are not sure enough of our experience. If the ch'i is allowed to become accelerating sha, fill this area with light and functional objects.

4 **South-east – children and family enrichment.** Good place to be if you like children. They may provoke you, though, with their messy habits – so remedy this provoking sha with lots of life and lots of colour.

5 **East – relationship enrichment.** The strongest yin
   enrichment in a yang location. If you enjoy and learn from
   growing within a relationship then this is a good area for you.
   Fill this area with movement and functional objects if you feel
   overwhelmed.

6 **North-east – friends and new beginnings enrichment.**
   A perfect place for you. This is where you should entertain all
   those friends of yours. Good place for your dining room. If the
   ch'i becomes stagnating sha, you'll have to remedy this area
   with colour and sound.

7 **North – pleasure and indulgence enrichment.** If your
   kitchen is in the east and your dining room in the north-east,
   then what could be better than having your sitting room here
   in the north? This location is very yin, nurturing and warm
   and here you can unwind. If the ch'i is allowed to linger here
   you'll never move. Remedies are to have movement and a
   beautiful piece of sculpture.

8 **North-west – health and happiness enrichment.** Watch
   your weight. The ch'i here is expansive and so could you, too,
   expand. To remedy this, fill the area with sound and straight
   lines. If the ch'i is allowed to become unpredictable sha who
   knows what could happen – it's unpredictable.

5

applying feng shui

In this chapter we apply the techniques and concepts of feng shui to the inside of your home. We'll look at its shape and what that can tell you, and then we'll look at each room in turn to see how you can get the maximum benefit from the feng shui. This is all done in some detail, to help make clear the interaction of ch'i flows, enrichments and remedies. When you have worked through the full process on your home, we hope that you will then feel able to apply the same techniques and concepts to other spaces and areas of your life. Apply feng shui to your garden, and you can match its various uses to its enrichments, correcting poor energy flows with remedies such as water features, plantings and screens. Apply feng shui to your office space, and to your desktop, to produce a more harmonious and productive working environment. The position of furniture and the use of light, colour, pot plants and mobile 'executive toys' may be appropriate remedies in an office.

The layout of your home

In Chapter 4 we talked about the PahKwa and about establishing which way your home faces. In order to work out the feng shui of your house, you now need to overlay the PahKwa on to a plan of your house. Take a plan – it can be fairly rough – and place the PahKwa over it so that the front door is in the fame enrichment of the PahKwa. You can now read off which enrichment each room or area falls into (see Figure 14).

If you are concerned about any particular aspect of your life, you now know which part of the house governs it. Suppose money is your big worry. If your wealth enrichment covers the bathroom, for example, this is clearly the room on which to concentrate.

Sometimes you may even be able to swap rooms around to improve things. Suppose one of your children has a tendency to ignore school work in favour of socializing, listening to music or any other form of enjoyment. Maybe their bedroom falls in the pleasure and indulgence enrichment, which is encouraging this lifestyle. Perhaps you could move them into the wisdom and experience enrichment, by swapping their room with the spare room, or with another child who is prone to be workaholic, or changing where they do their homework.

Some rooms are just too difficult or too expensive to move around, such as bathrooms and kitchens, in which case you can look for remedies within the rooms, as we shall see. But you can move most rooms around to place each in a more appropriate enrichment. You may be able to swap sitting rooms, dining rooms, bedrooms and studies around quite easily.

Missing sections

If your house is fairly square, you will find that the PahKwa sits comfortably on it. But if it's L-shaped, or T-shaped, or has a chunk out of one side, you may find that when you lay the PahKwa on the house plan there is an enrichment, or perhaps more than one, which doesn't have any part of your house within it.

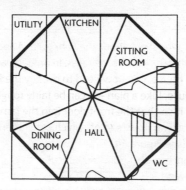

Figure 14 *Overlaying the PahKwa on to the house plan.*

These missing sections may indicate an aspect of your life which is missing or diminished in some way. For example, if your house contains no children and family enrichment, you may have no children, or those you have may be out of touch or living away from home. If you have no health and happiness enrichment, you may suffer poor health. A missing relationship enrichment might suggest you have no permanent relationship – either you are single or you have short-term relationships only.

Ideally, all eight enrichments should be roughly in balance; each should be about the same size. But unless your house is square, they won't be. A rectangular house will stretch the PahKwa shape when you overlay it, so that some enrichments are much larger than others. You will need to use feng shui to counter this imbalance.

You can, as always, remedy this; that's what feng shui is all about. The way to do it is to fill in the missing section of your house. This might sound impossible, but it is actually straightforward. Sometimes you can build on to the house, if you have the money and the space. You could add a conservatory to fill in the missing piece of an L-shaped house, or add an extension to fill in the space. But if this isn't possible, you can give the appearance that the missing piece is there by placing a mirror at the point where the missing section should begin (see Figure 15).

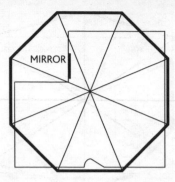

Figure 15 *Position a mirror to create a missing section or enlarge one that is too small.*

You can also use this technique to enlarge an enrichment that is too small. Suppose you are unhappy with your social life, and you have only a small section of your house within the friends and new beginnings enrichment. Place a mirror at a point where it will enlarge the friends and new beginnings enrichment, and you should find your social life improves as a result.

Extra sections

Rather than have missing sections, some houses have extra sections (and some have both). If your house is rectangular, you will need to stretch the PahKwa in two directions to fit on top of the plan (see Figure 16). This means that the enrichments which are extended are much larger than the others.

If an enrichment is particularly large, this means that you have an abundance of it. This may be a good thing, or it may not – only you can know. A large friends and new beginnings enrichment might be more than you can cope with – perhaps your social life is too demanding and you seem to attract an awful lot of friends whom you don't particularly want. In this case, you will need to do something to reduce the size of this section of your house. On the other hand, you may love having a big circle of friends and be more than happy with your social life – in which case don't change anything in this part of the house.

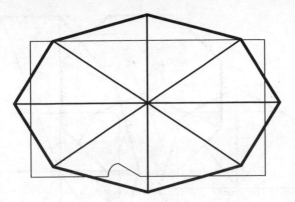

Figure 16 *Stretching the PahKwa to fit over a rectangular house.*

If you decide to reduce the influence of an enrichment, you should make this part of the house less dominant. Reduce the light levels, keep doors closed to prevent the ch'i circulating too much, or perhaps use straight-line remedies to discourage the ch'i from becoming too expansive. You may also be able to use this part of the house less, by swapping round the rooms you use. If your dining room is in this enrichment, for example, could you put a table in the kitchen and eat there more often, and save the dining room for special occasions only?

Building an extension

If you add on an extension to your house, you will affect its feng shui. Either you will fill in a missing enrichment or you will add an extra section on to one of the enrichments. Before you do this, you should draw up a plan of how your house is going to look with the new extension, and then lay the PahKwa on to it (see Figure 17). Work out where all the enrichments fall – it may affect the enrichments which other parts of the house fall into – and make sure you are happy with this layout before you go ahead and build.

Upstairs and downstairs

The PahKwa overlays all the floors of your house in the same way, so that any upstairs room will fall in the same enrichment

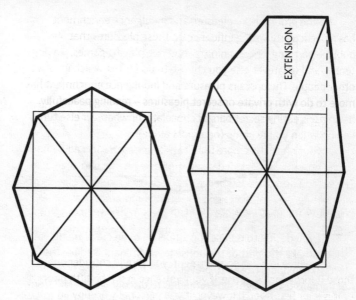

EXTENSION

Figure 17 *A new extension can change the enrichments into which other parts of the house fall.*

as the room beneath it. But suppose you have a larger ground floor than first floor if, for example, you have a single-storey kitchen extension? You might even have a larger upstairs. Some terraced houses have a section upstairs which protrudes into their neighbour's property.

If there is a section on one floor which is missing on another floor, you should rectify this. Either enlarge the missing section or reduce the extra section in the ways we have just looked at, in order to keep all the floors of the house in balance.

If your house has more than one storey, each one represents a slightly different aspect of yourself. The ground floor is yang, and represents the more open, obvious side of you which other people see and recognize. The first floor is more closely related to the private you – the side of you which only you, and perhaps your closest family and friends, tend to see.

So the ground floor pleasure and indulgence enrichment has a particularly strong influence on those pleasures that are public – partying, entertaining, eating out, playing games, playing tennis, and whatever else you choose to do for fun which involves other people. The upstairs pleasure and indulgence enrichment has more to do with private or secret pleasures – reading peacefully, having sex, eating secret bars of chocolate, or whatever else turns you on when you're alone (or almost alone).

If your house has more than two floors, each succeeding floor (going upwards) reflects a deeper and more private part of you. The second floor is concerned with the deeper intuitive aspects of your nature, and the attics will conceal the innermost part of you. If they are full of clutter and you never go into them, this indicates that you are not paying attention to the deeper and more spiritual aspects of yourself.

If you live in a flat or apartment, you should consider only those floors which you use. If your entrance is on the fifth floor, that is *your* first floor. (However, if you personally occupy an entire tower block, you will have a seriously multi-layered personality.)

General design

There are certain features that crop up in every room of the house, or almost every room, so we'll look at these first before we go through the house room by room. These features should be considered, whichever enrichment they fall into.

Windows and doors

Windows and doors are the entrances and exits to each room for the ch'i, so it is important that they should help it to flow in and out smoothly.

Windows

Windows should open outwards if possible, so the ch'i can get out as well as in. If the window faces west, it will let in unpredictable, often dangerous ch'i from the direction of the White Tiger. So these windows, especially, should never open inwards; it would be better not to open them at all.

Sash windows always block at least half of the window opening, even when they are fully open. If you cannot change the windows, you can encourage the ch'i in and out through the open half of the window by opening the lower part and placing a life or movement remedy on the window sill – a plant, perhaps, or an ornament which has movement, such as a Newton's cradle.

The shape of your windows is important because of the way it influences the ch'i as it enters. Square or roughly square windows are fine, but tall thin windows are harder for the ch'i to enter through. Ch'i loves round, octagonal and arched windows, but Gothic-style windows, which come to a point at the top, can be disruptive. You may get away with them if they face north, where they will wake up the sleepy Tortoise, but if they face west you will be provoking the already dangerous Tiger: don't take the risk. The Chinese often paint west-facing windows black to keep the Tiger out.

If you can't see out of the window clearly, the ch'i can't enter and leave easily. So avoid frosted glass unless you are trying to slow down ch'i, for example from the west. If the top of the window is too low to see through when you are standing up, this can cause depression, so make sure windows are set high enough.

An old house has its own character and personality, just as an old rock or tree does, and it is bad feng shui to damage it in any way. So you should never replace old windows with new ones (apart from repairing rotten windows with exact replicas). If your house has windows which open inwards, or are too small, or have Gothic arches to them, find remedies that don't involve tampering with the house's character. Use mirrors to encourage ch'i, wind chimes to slow it down, and rounded pelmets in front of pointed windows to smooth the flow of the ch'i.

Doors

The most important door is the front door, which we'll consider in a moment, but all the other doors in the house are important, too.

Enter each room in the house in turn and notice how you go through the door – the ch'i has to go the same way as you. Do you have to pull the door towards you in order to enter the room, or can you simply push it into the room? Are you greeted by a blank wall as you open the door, or does it open to give you a view of the whole room? Is your entrance blocked by a piece of furniture?

The door should be in proportion to the room. If it is too small, place a mirror inside the room to help the ch'i in; if it is too big, a wind chime will help to slow down the ch'i rushing out of it.

Your front door

The main link between the inside and the outside of your house is the front door. This is the main route in and out of the house not only for you, but also for the ch'i. So it's important that it should be right.

In order to make sure the front door is right, you have to consider what is outside it (we looked at this in Chapter 4). The ch'i arrives at the front door via whatever is outside it, and you need to think about whether this needs remedying. If there is too great a flow of ch'i – a long, straight, open path pointing at the door is in a dark, overgrown area where the ch'i is inclined to stagnate, you need to speed it up. If you live in a flat where the ch'i is rushing past your door and down a staircase, you need to encourage it to make a diversion and enter through your front door.

There are three key factors in the design of your front door which you can use to influence the ch'i:
* colour
* glass panelling
* pattern of decoration.

One way to change the effect of your front door is to change its colour. We've already looked at the effects of different colours and where to use them; paint the door a suitable colour to speed up or slow down the ch'i.

You can also add glass panelling to a solid door – or add a fanlight over it – to let more ch'i through. Equally, you could block in a glass panel to slow the ch'i down. You can add large or small glass panels, and use frosted or stained glass to calm the ch'i. Simply add or remove the right amount of glass to achieve the effect you need.

The decoration on the door, if you have any, will also influence the flow of ch'i. A round window or a curvy design will help the ch'i to flow gently. A pattern of straight lines – such as vertical planking – will speed up the ch'i since it is a straight-line remedy.

Think about the size of your front door. As with other doors, it should be in proportion to the front hall. If it is too small, position mirrors in the hall to make it appear larger. If it is too big, on the other hand, hang a wind chime just inside it to prevent the ch'i rushing in too fast.

As with everything else, the front door should be kept clean, the paint should be refreshed frequently, and any damage should be repaired promptly. Lights outside the door help to encourage ch'i, but make sure you always replace blown bulbs straight away. The area around the front door, inside and out, should be kept free of clutter.

Entering through a different door

Some people tend to enter their house through the back door, or through a side door, instead of using the front door. If you fall into this category, what does it mean in terms of feng shui? It doesn't alter the direction the house faces, which tells you how to lay the PahKwa on to it. But it does make a lot of difference to which enrichment you enter through.

The front door always – by definition – falls in the fame enrichment, which governs your public face and how you appear to the world. By avoiding the front door you are avoiding this aspect of yourself and your life. You may be a private person, who sees your home as an escape and a refuge from the outside world. You are not making use of the interface between the outer world and the home world, which suggests that you like to keep your public and private lives separate.

So which enrichment are you entering through? Presumably through one in which you are very much at home. If the door you typically use is in the pleasure and indulgence enrichment, for example, it is likely that you entertain a lot and enjoy relaxing at home – you see your house as somewhere to enjoy yourself, rather than as a place full of chores or loneliness.

Or perhaps you use a door in the health and happiness enrichment. If this is the case you are probably health conscious. Perhaps you frequently diet, or make a point of eating healthy food. You probably take plenty of exercise, use vitamin supplements and have an interest in health matters generally. You are likely to have a complementary medical practitioner of some kind whom you often visit – an osteopath, acupuncturist, homoeopath or reflexologist.

Establish in which enrichment the door you normally use is. Whichever it is, you will find that it is in an area that is particularly important to you, and probably in a positive way.

Walls and ceilings

A large, smooth, blank wall is discouraging to ch'i; ch'i simply rushes straight past it. So make your walls interesting to slow the ch'i down by hanging pictures or displaying ornaments. If you need to liven up the ch'i, you could add a dado or picture rail, but since these are straight-line remedies you should avoid them in rooms where the ch'i is already lively, and especially in the west.

If you live in an old house which already has these period features in rooms where the ch'i doesn't need to be any more lively, you shouldn't damage the character of the house by removing the dado or picture rails. Instead, soften the effect of the straight lines with rounded and curvy ornaments – such as plates hung above the picture rail. You can also help by breaking the line of the rail; a sofa with a high, rounded back positioned against a wall with a dado rail, will come up above the dado and break the line.

A cornice around the top of the walls is excellent since it prevents the ch'i getting stuck in the corner between the walls and the ceiling. If you are adding the cornice, choose a design that has a curvy profile.

If you use patterned wallpaper on the walls, choose a subtle pattern or you will distract the ch'i away from the rest of the room. Patterns with curving or rounded shapes are better for feng shui than square or checked designs.

The height of the ceiling should be in proportion to the room. If it's too low, raise it visually by painting it a lighter colour than the walls. Conversely, if it is too high, paint it a darker colour than the walls.

If your ceilings slope, this is good for helping the ch'i to flow harmoniously. However, if the bottom of the slope finishes below eye level, don't spend much time below it. This is not the place to put a bed, a sofa or a desk. Use the space for storage, keeping books or displaying ornaments.

Beams

If you live in a house with exposed beams, you need to pay these special attention. They are straight lines which can funnel ch'i until it becomes dangerously accelerated; the Chinese avoid them, but in the West they are popular. There are three main action points for improving the feng shui of a beamed house.

* **Tone down the colour contrast between the beams and the ceiling.** Black beams against a white ceiling draw the ch'i to the beams, which is what you want to avoid. Strip the beams of paint or stain so that they are a less strident, more natural colour. You can also paint the ceiling off-white or even, perhaps, a darker colour so the beams create less of a contrast. In some beamed houses you can paint the beams themselves without detracting from the character of the house – an old boathouse with a beamed wooden ceiling, for example, could be painted pale blue or off-white throughout.

* **Break up the line of the beams.** Hang ribbons or wind chimes on the beams or, if you want a less oriental look, hang wicker baskets or old china jugs (but not dried flowers – anything dead is bad feng shui). You can also use a straight-line remedy, surprisingly; place bamboo flutes – or similar straight objects – across the beam at an angle of 45 degrees. Put a bamboo flute at each end of the beam, about a third of the way in from the wall. One end of the flute should point at the ceiling and the other at the wall. The effect of this is to cut across the corner where the

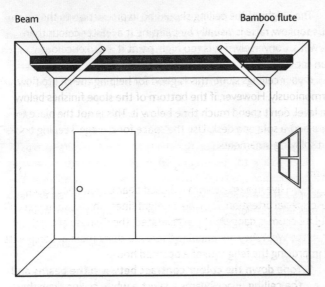

Figure 18 *Break up the straight line of a beam by hanging bamboo flutes across it.*

wall and ceiling meet, and at the same time to create the top half of a PahKwa (see Figure 18).

* **Avoid spending a lot of time beneath a beam.** Don't place any furniture which you spend a lot of time on, such as a bed or favourite chair, under a beam. You should also avoid positioning the cooker or sink under a beam, or any other piece of furniture or equipment that you use regularly.

Colour in the house

Different colours are suitable in different parts of the house, depending on which way the house faces and where the ch'i in that area is coming from. In the west of the house, for example, you would use different colours from those you would use in the east. In each part of the house, you should choose your palette according to whether you want to encourage or slow down the ch'i.

You should also take into account your own element – or the element of the person who most often uses the room. The colours which are appropriate to your element will always be suitable for a room that you use. If, for example, you are a strongly water person, you will probably be horrified at the thought of using bright purple, orange or red to liven up the ch'i in the south area of your house. However, you can use a bright blue (which is an enlivening water colour) instead.

If you need to liven up the ch'i with bright colours such as purple or yellow, this doesn't mean you have to paint all the walls in a garish purple. You could use a more neutral (but still lively) colour such as a yellowy ivory on the walls, and then use flashes of purple in cushions, rugs and curtains, and in the decoration. You might have a vase containing plum-coloured ostrich feathers, a pair of purple glass candlesticks, or a pile of cream, lilac, and purple hat boxes on top of a cupboard.

The following chart shows which element and which colours are appropriate for each direction. So, for example, fire is the element which is at home in the south. In south rooms, or in any part of the house predominantly used by a fire person (see Chapter 3 to establish your own element), reds, purples, oranges and yellows will strengthen ch'i. If you need to damp down the effects of the ch'i, you can use green.

Direction	Element	Colours to encourage ch'i	Colours to slow down ch'i
South or south-east	Fire	Purple, red, orange, yellow	Green
North	Water	Bright blue and black, or white and gold	Soft, muted blue
East or north-east	Wood	Green	Blue and black
West or north-west	Metal	Gold and white	Brown and earthy yellow such as ochre
South-west	Earth	Earthy brown and yellow	Soft deep red, lilac

Rooms and their feng shui

We've already established that the feng shui of each room is determined by various factors, such as the direction it faces and the enrichment in which it falls. But there are additional factors that are specific to each type of room, and we're going to look at these now.

The hall

The hall is the first room you enter when you come in through the front door, so it is also the room the ch'i first enters. It is critical that you invite the ch'i in, and then encourage it to circulate so that it can go on to reach all the rest of the house. A stagnating hall, one which is poky or dark, can have a damaging effect on the entire house by preventing the ch'i from flowing harmoniously before it has even begun.

We've already seen how the size of the hall and the front door should be in proportion to each other. If the door is too large, you can slow down the ch'i with a wind chime or banner hung just inside it. But generally, the hall should encourage the ch'i in. It isn't a place to sit and relax; it's a place for coming and going and bustle and activity, so you want a good lively flow of ch'i.

Remove any clutter from your hall. If you simply can't put it anywhere else, buy or build a cupboard to hide it in. Paint the hall a light, bright, welcoming colour, appropriate to the direction it faces. Hang a mirror to make it appear larger and brighter. If it is small, hang the mirror opposite the front door; if it is large, hang the mirror at right angles to the door. If the hall is long and thin, hang a mirror on one of the long walls.

Many front halls, especially in flats, don't have windows. In this case, you must make a special effort to brighten up the area and put a high wattage bulb in the light. If you do have a window, keep the curtains well drawn back during the day to let in the maximum light; make opening the curtains the first job you do when you come downstairs in the morning, and do it with a flourish to let in the light and the ch'i.

If the stairs dominate the hall, don't box them in but have open banisters so the ch'i can flow in and out. If the stairs face the door, there is a danger that the ch'i will run straight down them and out through the door, so you need to slow it down. If you have room, put a screen between the bottom of the stairs and the front door. Otherwise hang a wind chime or ribbon from the ceiling between the stairs and the front door.

Stairs

Ch'i travels up and down stairs just as we do, so it needs to be encouraged to do so freely and easily. Staircases should be as wide as possible, so keep them free from clutter and mess. Don't use them for storing shoes, books or anything else. Don't have a door at the top or bottom of the stairs or the ch'i will be unable to move to the next floor; if you already have such a door either remove it or leave it permanently open. Avoid open-tread stairs since these help the ch'i to flow down and around, but discourage it from flowing upwards.

Straight runs of stairs can speed the ch'i up too much, so slow it down with wind chimes hung above them. Stairs with a lot of twists and turns have the opposite effect – the ch'i stagnates – so help it down by hanging mirrors at the bends, or even by painting a flowing mural design on the wall for it to follow.

Corridors and landings

The wider and brighter your corridors and landings are, the better. Use mirrors to make them seem wider if necessary, and keep some of the doors which lead off them open to let in more light and give a greater feeling of space. Break up long, narrow corridors by hanging wind chimes, banners, or some other object which will slow down the ch'i, from the ceiling.

If a corridor is short you can lengthen it by hanging a mirror at one or both ends to open it up and help the ch'i to flow more smoothly along and around it. It will also help to open the doors which lead off it.

The way doors are aligned in corridors is important. If two opposite doors are not quite aligned, you should remedy this with a mirror beside each which reflects the section of the opposite door that projects out. If two opposite doors are of different sizes, the larger one should lead to the more important room. If this isn't the case, a mirror on the large door will reflect the smaller one and make it seem larger.

If a long corridor or landing has a door at the end, facing back down the corridor, the ch'i will be funnelled towards it. Hang wind chimes along the corridor and outside the door, or some other object which will slow down the ch'i.

Doors which open so that they hit each other are very bad feng shui, and will cause conflict in whatever enrichment they fall. Re-hang one of the doors to prevent this, or replace it with narrow double doors which don't reach as far as the other door.

Kitchens

For many people, the kitchen is the most important room in the house – the heart of the home. If you can, site it in an enrichment which is suitable for you. If it is in your health and happiness enrichment, it will be an excellent place to cook good, healthy food. It is well suited to the wealth enrichment, too, because the Chinese words for food and wealth sound similar.

If the kitchen is in the pleasure and indulgence enrichment, you will find that you entertain in there a lot. In this position, and with a kitchen large enough to have a table you can eat at, you will probably find that an evening's entertaining starts and ends in the kitchen, and never goes near the sitting room. With this arrangement, you need not bother with a dining room – use the room for something else.

The kitchen should be light and bright, with no dark corners. If necessary, use mirrors or lights to brighten up any dead areas. You can also use light or reflective materials such as stainless steel for cookers and pale marble (if you can afford it) for work surfaces. At least you could have a marble slab sitting on a work surface, which is ideal for making pastry as well as for lightening up a dull area.

An untidy kitchen makes for bad feng shui, so make sure everything has its place and is regularly tidied away; at least, make yourself tidy up every night before you go to bed. Use vegetable baskets, spice shelves, racks inside cupboard doors, and anything else to enable you to keep food, spices, crockery and pots and pans off the work surfaces and out of the way.

One of the most important considerations in the kitchen is that when you are working in there, you should be able to see anyone entering or leaving the room. So try to avoid a layout that means you have your back to the door when you are at the sink, cooker or work surface. If you can't avoid this, at least you can place a mirror so that you can see the door reflected in it (see Figure 19).

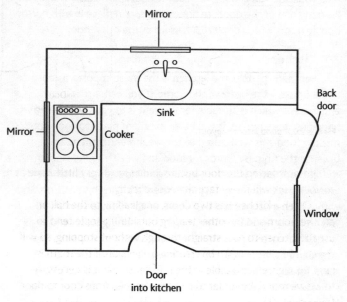

Figure 19 *A poor kitchen layout, remedied using mirrors.*

In an ideal layout, the cooker and the sink should not be next to each other, since they represent the elements of fire and water, which don't combine well (see Figure 20). Separate them as far as possible, and place a wooden object between the two of them, such as a chopping board or a wicker vegetable basket. You can site the

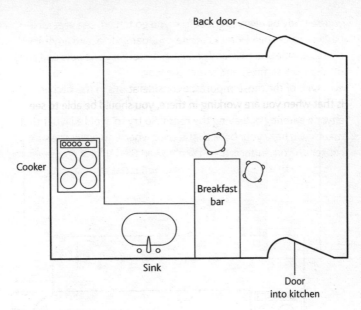

Figure 20 *A good kitchen layout.*

refrigerator facing the door because you spend very little time at it, so your back will rarely face the door directly.

Often a kitchen has two doors, one leading to the hall or another room and the other leading outside. If people tend to use the kitchen to pass straight through without stopping, so will the ch'i. So slow it down by creating a diversion. If the room is large enough, place a table in the middle so that it is necessary to weave round it in order to cross the kitchen from door to door (see Figure 21).

Sitting rooms

Think about which enrichment this room falls in. Is it a suitable one such as pleasure and indulgence or friends and new beginnings? If you spend most of your rest time with your children (if this isn't a contradiction in terms), a sitting room in the children and family

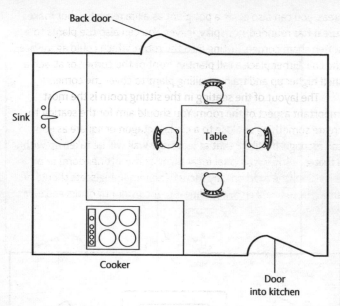

Figure 21 *A strategically placed kitchen table will slow the ch'i down if the kitchen is used as a corridor.*

enrichment would be suitable. If you spend a lot of time alone and like to sit and read, the wisdom enrichment might be good for your sitting room.

If your sitting room is not in the enrichment you would like it to be, and you can't swap your rooms around, introduce a remedy that would suit the enrichment you would like for your sitting room. For example, if you would like it to be in your friends and new beginnings enrichment, choose remedies that suit this enrichment. Sound remedies are the best for your friends and new beginnings enrichment, so put a chiming clock or a CD player in the sitting room to represent the friends and new beginnings enrichment.

As always, make sure this room is bright and has no dead corners or alcoves. As well as using colour and light to lift these areas, you can also place a pot plant as a life remedy – but make sure it has rounded, not spiky, leaves. You can also use plants to soften sharp corners jutting into the room, which could aggravate the ch'i. Either place a tall plant in front of the corner, or attach a shelf higher up and train a trailing plant to cover the corner.

The layout of the seating in the sitting room is the most important aspect of the room. You should aim for the seating to create something as close to a circle, octagon or square as you can manage. It's likely that at least one wall will be taken up with a fireplace (the traditional focal point of the sitting room) or a television (the modern-day focus). The remaining seats should be arranged to avoid creating a line-up or corridor of chairs and sofas (see Figure 22).

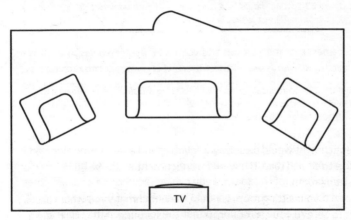

Figure 22 *A poor sitting room layout where the seating creates a corridor.*

The sitting room should not be cluttered with furniture, or the ch'i cannot flow around it. So make sure the amount of furniture, and its size, suits the proportions of the room. A mirror in the room, preferably above the fireplace, will help to create a feeling of space (see Figure 23).

There is one seat in the room, or occasionally more than one, which is known by the Chinese as 'honoured guest' position. This is

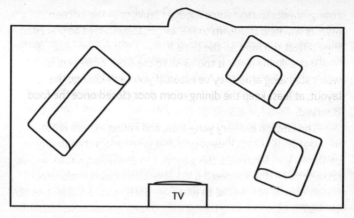

Figure 23 *Seating should be arranged around four sides, or three if the fourth side accommodates the fireplace or television.*

the best seat in the room and you can tell which one it is because everyone always wants to sit there. It is always comfortable and it faces the door so that its occupant is in control of who enters and leaves the room. You can't spring any surprises on the person in honoured guest position.

Dining rooms

As with the kitchen and sitting rooms, find a suitable enrichment for this room if you can, or incorporate a remedy that suits the enrichment you would have chosen if you could.

Arrange the furniture so that the focus is on the table, and the food when it is spread out on it. The table should be oval or round if possible; square tables are acceptable but long, thin tables funnel the ch'i and create an atmosphere in which it is difficult to relax.

Make sure there is plenty of room to open the door and walk around the table and chairs without feeling cramped. If you can't do this you need a smaller table. If this means you haven't room for all the friends you like to entertain, don't cram them into an over-full room or they'll all end up with indigestion. Change your arrangements so that you eat buffet style, or in the kitchen. Mirrors will help the room to feel larger; they should be placed so they reflect the food on the table.

If the dining room is too close to the front door, people won't stay long after they've eaten. If you can't change the layout, at least keep the dining room door closed once the food is served.

The kitchen is a very yang area, and eating in here is not necessarily relaxing. However, if what you want is stimulating conversation over meals, this may not matter to you. You can also relax better in the kitchen if it is in the pleasure and indulgence enrichment. If you do like to entertain in the kitchen, create a more yin feel to it by lowering the lighting once the food is served. Either put the lights on a dimmer switch, or turn off the main light and use only table lights.

Utility rooms

These rooms are full of energy, with machines buzzing and whirring and clanking, and stirring up the ch'i. If you possibly can, locate this room in the east of the house, where the gentle ch'i from the Green Dragon will be able to cope. Or locate the room in the wisdom and experience enrichment, traditionally governed by the Green Dragon, where mechanical devices are most at home.

Even so, wherever you site the room, you need to keep it as calm as possible to counteract all that frenetic energy. The bigger the room, the more scope there is for the ch'i to circulate and dissipate the energy. Use a restful colour in this room; paint it a soft blue or green, or a pastel shade, to suit its direction.

Try to avoid lining up the machines opposite or alongside each other; stagger them as much as possible. A clothes airer down the centre of a long room, or across a wider one, will help to slow down the ch'i as it has to negotiate all the damp clothes (see Figure 24). However, a clothes airer creates a straight line, so soften this by hanging the clothes irregularly across and along it when you can, rather than accentuating the lines with clothes hung in regimented rows.

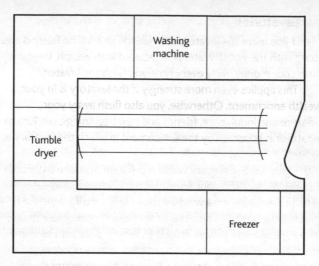

Figure 24 *The machines in this utility room are placed to spread their energy around the room, and the clothes on the airer help to slow down the ch'i further.*

Bathrooms

You should always be able to see the door from the bath, shower, lavatory or basin. If you can't, place a mirror in a position where it reflects the door. The room should be as uncluttered as possible, so make sure you have plenty of cupboards and shelves on which to store everything.

A bathroom is used to invigorate and refresh, but also to relax and wind down, so make sure you can do both in your bathroom. Decorate it in bright, fresh, clean colours, but place low lighting or candles so that you can turn the main light off and relax if you need to.

It is bad feng shui for the first view when you open the door to be of the lavatory. If you can't move the lavatory, screen it off, perhaps with a towel rail protruding from the wall. Sometimes, re-hanging the door to hinge on the other side does the trick. If you can't manage this either, hang a wind chime just inside the door as a distraction. The bathroom door should be kept closed when the room is not being used.

Lavatories

If you leave the lavatory seat up, the ch'i will be flushed away along with the water. Water is associated with wealth, so you will flush your money away every time you flush the lavatory.

This applies even more strongly if the lavatory is in your wealth enrichment. Otherwise, you also flush away your pleasure and indulgence, friends and new beginnings, wisdom or whatever is governed by the enrichment in which the lavatory is located.

If you have a lavatory which is separate from the bathroom, it shouldn't face the door. However, this is often unavoidable. In this case, you want a window above the lavatory, which you should keep bright and inviting. If the view is good, make it easy to see (people can always draw the curtains once they're in the room). If the view is poor, put a pot plant on the windowsill. If there is no window above the lavatory, hang a mirror there instead.

Bedrooms

It's vital to get the feng shui of your bedroom right; after all, you spend more time there than anywhere else. Do your best to make sure your bedroom falls in an enrichment which is right for you – ideally, pleasure and indulgence, relationship or health and happiness. If it doesn't, swap with another room if you possibly can. Otherwise, bring in remedies which suit the enrichment you would like your bedroom to be in. It is also a good idea to have a bedroom that faces in the direction which suits your personal element:

* fire: south or south-east
* water: north
* wood: east or north-east
* metal: west or north-west
* earth: south-west.

If you can't manage to get your bedroom into the right enrichment or facing the right way, there is one more thing you should be able to manage. Lay the PahKwa over your bedroom only, with the fame enrichment over the direction the room faces, and see which part of the room to put the bed in – either a suitable enrichment within the room, or in the direction which suits your own element. If you're not sure which way the room faces, use your intuition. Most rooms face the window, but sometimes you sense that a room faces the door, especially if there are no windows, or the windows are very small, or if the door is particularly large.

Position the bed so that you can easily see people entering and leaving through the door (see Figure 25). Don't point the foot of the bed directly at the door: dead people are laid out like that before being carried out feet first. If you can't see the door easily from the bed – and you can't reposition the bed – hang a mirror so the door is reflected in it when you lie in bed.

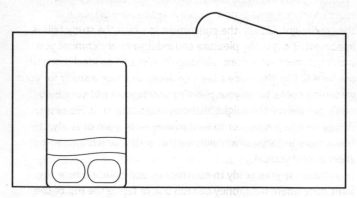

Figure 25 *This is a suitable arrangement for a bedroom, in which the bed does not face the door directly, but has a clear view of it.*

The bed should not sit directly underneath a light, as this is bad feng shui. The energy from the light, even when it is off, is disruptive when you are trying to sleep. If you can't change this arrangement, at least make sure the light is never used, and use a side light instead.

The bed itself needs the ch'i to flow over, around and under it. This means that a bed which sits on the floor with no space under

it is bad feng shui as it prevents the ch'i from flowing beneath it.
Use a bed in the old-fashioned style which sits well clear of the
floor. You should use a headboard, even if it is simply attached
to the wall and not to the bed at all. Choose one that suits your
personal element:

* fire: angular in shape and in a bright colour
* water: a curvy shape and coloured blue or green
* wood: squared and wooden
* metal: steel, iron or brass
* earth: use natural rather than synthetic materials in natural,
  unbleached and undyed colours

The study

Many homes have a study, whether they double up as a
spare room or a dining room, or are a dedicated workplace in
their own right. Clearly, the enrichment in which the study falls is
important; if it is in the pleasure and indulgence enrichment you
won't get much work done, although it might be an ideal room to
use for a hobby. If you are a keen gardener and have a study for your
gardening books, to do your planning and to work out your bulb
catalogue orders, this might be the perfect place for it. However,
if you use it to pay bills or to earn money, or to learn or study,
find a more suitable enrichment such as wealth or wisdom and
experience if you can.

If you use your study to earn money, don't place it near the
front door where the money can run out, or facing the top of the
stairs where it will run down the stairs. If you really can't move it,
keep the door shut, especially when you're working.

Often, a study is part of another room such as a sitting room
or bedroom. This is fine, but try to choose a room in a suitable
enrichment. In any case lay the PahKwa on to the room alone and
work out which is the wealth or wisdom and experience enrichment
within the room and place the desk there. As we saw before, you'll
need to establish which way the room faces. Most face the window,
but you can sense that some rooms face the door if it is much more
dominant than the window.

Balance the two uses of the room, in terms of both space and lighting. Don't cram a tiny study into the corner of a large dining room, or into the tiny space under the hall stairs. Cramped studies don't give your wealth or your intellect room to expand. Make sure that a well-lit study area is balanced by good lighting in the rest of the room.

The desk itself is important. You shouldn't sit with your back to a door; if you can't avoid it, hang a mirror above the desk. However short of space you are, have the largest desk you can manage; you don't want to be cramped. Always keep the desk tidy and free from clutter.

Creating good feng shui in your home isn't difficult; it just requires thought and a methodical approach. If you feel your house needs a huge amount of work, simply tackle one area at a time, starting with the enrichments you feel are most important, and work through the house a stage at a time. Or you could tackle the new beginnings enrichment first, to help get you started. Before you've finished, you'll already have started to feel the benefits of the first changes – and that will give you the encouragement you need to keep going.